CONTEMPORARY

FRENCH

LITERATURE

1945 AND AFTER

GAËTAN PICON

Frederick Ungar Publishing Co.   New York

Translated from the French manuscript
by Kelvin W. Scott and Graham D. Martin

C C

PUBLISHER'S NOTE

To enhance the usefulness of *Contemporary French Literature* as a reference work, each author's dates are given at his first appearance in the book, and there is an index of authors at the end. In addition, the title of a literary work is given in French at the first appearance, followed by the date of publication and a literal English translation; thereafter, the literal translation is used. In the back of the book is a listing of published English translations of the works mentioned.

CONTENTS

INTRODUCTION

French literature since 1945 has offered a great many
serious works, and some masterpieces. Its failure to measure up to the period between the two world wars should
be seen as part of a more general trend, not as something
peculiar to France. At any rate, French literature since
World War II has overcome one of its less attractive
traits—a sense of superiority that isolated it to some
extent from other literatures. Now, no longer ignoring the
existence of other literatures, French writers have become
receptive to influences of all kinds, especially the American novel (Faulkner, Hemingway, Dos Passos), German
philosophy (Heidegger), German and Spanish drama
(Brecht and García Lorca), and early twentieth-century
fiction (Kafka, Joyce, James) that had been admired but
not emulated. Although some have claimed that French
literature is in a state of decline, it still maintains its high
reputation: it is the most translated and most written
about of all European literatures, and it holds the record
number of Nobel Prizes (six since 1945).

Social conditions have been favorable for French literature since World War II. A wider public has appeared
through increased access to education, through inexpen-
sive paperback books, through radio and television. At
the same time, the prohibitions that used to restrict

certain areas of literature, or reserve them for a privileged few, have been more-or-less removed. A few regrettable acts of censorship should not make us forget that the freedom French literature enjoys today is unprecedented. The most daring and most difficult works are immediately acknowledged and commented on, and the most recent and topical works are studied in the universities.

But the spread of literature in France has gone hand in hand with a growing commercialization that treats books more and more like consumer goods. Advertising, the ever-increasing number of literary prizes, the role of the publicity agent—the new intermediary between the publisher and the critic—have all tended to stress the product most likely to succeed; and the part played by the critic, the bookseller, and ultimately the reader himself has lost importance. Hence the tendency for sales to concentrate on a few new titles, to the detriment of less immediately successful works and the publisher's backlist.

Moreover, the removal of prohibitions has proved a spur not so much to daring as to indifference toward a literature which is no longer under attack and which the revolutionaries renounce as being immediately appropriated by the society they condemn. The extent and immediacy of the spread of literature have created a kind of saturation, which represents a threat to its value and durability, and literature has defended itself by becoming more and more difficult and more and more intellectual, striving after refinements that ultimately are intended only for the eyes of other writers, and engaging in a self-analysis suitable only for literary theorists. The erosion of literature's most immediate powers by motion pictures and television has also contributed to this elitist tendency.

Infinitely more subtle than twentieth-century literature before World War II, French literature of recent years is, nonetheless, less fertile and less alive. It is no longer characterized by a wide diversity of creative tempera- ments, of writers who give pleasure to the reader, but rather by dominant lines of thought, each wanting to be exclusive. A work of literature used to go beyond con- sciousness; today consciousness tends to be an end in itself. We have witnessed a double reduction: the writer has been reducing diversity to the unity of a formula, and the critic has been reducing the work to its structure.

As a result, it has never been easier to divide literature into currents, which represent not so much similarities of sensibility and talent as a common intellectual attitude. In this respect, nothing is more revealing than the change in the role and formula of the literary journal. The journal which was an anthology of the best writers, which drew its strength from its very variety, has disappeared. At- tempts to fight against this trend have been doomed to failure: the *Nouvelle revue française* is languishing, and the *Mercure de France* has disappeared (I was its last director, from 1963 to 1966). The journals of today are, like Jean-Paul Sartre's (born 1905) *Les temps modernes*, committed to a philosophical political doctrine or, like *Tel Quel* or *Change*, to a theoretical political doctrine or, like *Critique*, to a purely analytical approach. Even critics writing for weekly magazines have lost their former subtlety and personal approach; they either totally accept or totally reject, and they judge works of literature ac- cording to their own formulas. In other words, they are ideologically conditioned.

The literature surveyed in this book is but a very small

part of what is printed and read. Sociologists—who define literature solely in terms of what is printed and read— question the legitimacy of any distinction between literature and *paraliterature* or *subliterature*; but sociologists' definitions are not mine. The literature I will discuss is easily distinguishable, even though it includes both best-selling authors and writers whose work is much talked about but sells badly (before Samuel Beckett [born 1906] was awarded the Nobel Prize, his novels sold fewer than a thousand copies each). This literature forms a coherent whole within which the works of individual writers can be interrelated, thus implying a concept of literature that either unites them or places them in opposition to each other. It is not writing intended for immediate and transient consumption, but writing that calls for criticism and analysis; it is read and studied throughout the world (readership abroad, it is said, is the contemporary equivalent of posterity); and it aspires, if not to eternity, at least to some kind of duration, taking its place—at least provisionally—in history.

THE HERITAGE

The literature of today is so far removed from prewar literature that we sometimes have to make an effort to remember that prewar writers continued to publish in the years following the liberation. Yet, 1945 did not mark a sudden break. Each year there were tenuous, imperceptible breaks, one slight shift after another, although their overall effect now strikes us as amounting to an almost radical contrast.

Indeed, sometimes we have to remind ourselves that three writers who can be described as the last great classicists concluded their careers between 1940 and 1955. A year before his death Paul Valéry (1871–1945) published *Propos me concernant* (1944, Remarks about Myself), an outline of an intellectual biography embodying the features of his character-persona Monsieur Teste, and the last volume of *Variété* (1924–44, Variety). And his unfinished play *"Mon Faust"* (1946, "My Faust"), which might have been one of his masterpieces, was published soon after his death. In the last years of his life Paul Claudel (1868–1955) published *Présence et prophétie* (1942, Presence and Prophecy), *L'histoire de Tobie et de Sara* (1942, The Story of Tobias and Sara), and various

fragments of a biblical commentary, which, taken together, constitute one of his major works. And André
Gide (1869–1951) published, in addition to the last part
of his often monotonous *Journal* (1950, Journal), a very
fine novella, *Thésée* (1946, Theseus), which ends with
a serene farewell and testament:

> I have no regrets as my solitary death draws near.
> I have enjoyed the benefits of the earth. It is pleas-
> ant for me to think that, after me, and thanks to
> me, men will find themselves happier, better, and
> freer. For the good of future humanity, I have lived.

These three writers can be called the last great classicists
not only because none of their successors has attained
the same stature but also because the concept of literature
has radically changed; and it may well be that there is a
relationship between their "classic" concept of literature
and the possibility of personal greatness.

It is not easy to pinpoint when the break occurred.
Consider, however, the preface written by Gide in 1949
for his *Anthologie de la poésie française* (Anthology of
French Poetry), in which he gave a disillusioned testament:

> I used to write before the war, "I shall win my case
> only on appeal" or "I write to be reread." But such
> statements will mean nothing when there is no
> longer any appeal and no longer any question of
> rereading. Only shock and surprise will then have
> the power to move. . . . At a stroke, there will be
> the end of our culture and of the tradition we have
> fought so long to maintain.

Gide felt that tradition was dying, but by whose hand he was not sure. The taste for shock and surprise, which Gide detected after the war and which Valéry denounced in his poetics and Claudel in his continual indictment of modernity, was not the fundamental cause of the break. The rupture was primarily due to a lack of faith in literature. The last classical writers (including Thomas Mann as well as Gide, Valéry, and Claudel) believed in literature. It is true that only for Gide was literary creation, in its limited perfection, an absolute; for Claudel it was a form of prayer; and for Valéry, an example of the power of language, whose anonymous faculties of creation and transformation fascinated him infinitely more than any personal achievement. But prayer must be as beautiful as possible, and the same is true of linguistic exercises, in prose or in poetry; God, or a saint ("Honor of men, Sainted Language," wrote Valéry), must be fittingly served, and in so doing the beauty of literature keeps meaning intact. Thus, although their art represented a considerable innovation at the beginning of the twentieth century, and although within its limits their work was always subordinated to the value it expressed and served (even for Gide it expressed and served "man"), these writers never challenged the concept of literature itself: its function was accepted, and its tradition was venerated.

The period after World War II has seen the development of two very different literary movements. The first, the existentialist, is a literature of *content*, which, by using simplified, sometimes slipshod means and a style of writing that is sometimes colorless, expresses a particular view of man and the universe. The second, the formalist or structuralist, seems to be interested only in *structure*, without worrying too much about what it expresses and even at times going so far as to say that there is nothing to express—that there is no meaning. Despite their differences, both existentialism and formalism have undermined the traditional definition of literature as a relationship between form and content, a relationship to which the last great classicist works owed their strength.

One of the characteristics of the three last great classicists, however, was the diversity of the genres they encompassed and sometimes mixed so freely that, although the concept of literature was not challenged, at least the concept of genres was; Gide, Claudel, and Valéry can be categorized only as writers. But this is not to say that other writers of the early twentieth century abandoned traditional genres, or that they have even disappeared today (though they may be somewhat played out). Just as there is *the* drama, there is *the* novel. And the novel has been regarded as a superior and immutable genre, whose success in the nineteenth century has encouraged writers to devote themselves to it exclusively without making much of an effort to modify its laws.

Novels of this kind—the sort of literature most eagerly and widely read by the general public, it is encouraged by large printings and by prizes such as the Prix Goncourt and the Prix Femina—are primarily stories portraying characters in a social and geographical setting. Although in depicting this setting the author reveals his own vision of things, it is understood that the fictional "reality" must reflect a psychological or sociological truth. The novel must instruct as it diverts; it persuades the reader that what is fictional is true, and the art of the narrator is judged by the extent to which he is successful in creating this illusion.

In fiction before World War II, Jules Romains (1885–1972), Roger Martin du Gard (1881–1958), Georges Duhamel (1884–1966), and François Mauriac (1885–1970) were masters of a narrative tradition that included the sociological epic in the form of vast novel cycles, and the psychological tragedy condensed into a short novel of about two hundred pages. (The word *récit* is frequently used in French to designate such short novels.) This tradition persisted after the war and is still with us today, but it has not found the same masters.

Either because they were growing old or because their confidence was to some extent shaken by the new atmosphere, the four masters cited above added nothing decisive to their work. At his death in 1958, Roger Martin du Gard left thousands of pages of a huge novel that was much more personal than his earlier works—*Souvenirs du Colonel de Maumort* (Reminiscences of Colonel de Maumort)—which has not yet been published. The manuscript contains some very fine moments—in particular an admirable episode entitled *La baignade* (The Bathing Place), but perhaps it was no accident that the author was unable to put it into its final form. Aware that traditional techniques were worn out, Martin du Gard attempted in *Reminiscences of Colonel de Maumort* a first-person narrative in a mode very different from the objectivity of *Les Thibault* (1922–40, The Thibault Family), but he did not succeed in mastering it.

After a long period during which he wrote no novels, François Mauriac temporarily abandoned his political journalism to write *Un adolescent d'autrefois* (1969, An

Adolescent of Former Times). But this novel was not up to the standard of such earlier novels as *Le Nœud de vipères* (1932, The Nest of Vipers), and he wrote it only because the student riots of May, 1968, prompted the old writer to look back on his own youth. Mauriac, too, was unable to accept the way in which the novel had begun to evolve even before the war, and he was greatly inhibited by the changes.

Apart from the traditional novel—which followed the lines laid down by the great masters of the nineteenth century, from Honoré de Balzac (1799–1850) to Guy de Maupassant (1850–1893)— there had developed after World War I a literature that was markedly original in spirit and in form. A poetic and imaginative fiction, receptive to the play of language, shifted the boundaries separating the genres; it reflected the euphoric easing of tensions after World War I and celebrated the modern world greeted so magnificently by Guillaume Apollinaire's (1880–1918) poem *Zone* (1913, Zone). This prose included the "novels" of such writers as Max Jacob (1876–1944), Valéry Larbaud (1881–1957), Jean Giraudoux (1882–1944), Blaise Cendrars (1887–1961, Paul Morand (born 1888), Jean Cocteau (1889–1943), Joseph Delteil (born 1894), Philippe Soupault (born 1897), and René Crevel (1900–1935), storytellers who were often also writers of verse. Their works belong to a world that has disappeared, a world of luxury and ease that the anguish of today rejects. Yet Paul Morand, with *Venises* (1971, Venices), a nostalgic evocation of a city he has known and loved for half a century, recently reminded us of his exquisite mastery as a writer. And the posthumous publication of an unfinished novel by Giraudoux, *La menteuse*

(1969, Lying Woman), prevents us from too easily dismissing a writer who, as the novelist and critic Maurice Blanchot (born 1907) rightly saw, was one of the first to free the novel from its subjugation to realism and to identify it with the movement of the language itself, through which invention is given free rein.

The heritage of the period between the two wars includes one movement—surrealism—that warrants special mention because it continues to exercise its sway. The whole of modern poetry, in its self-awareness and its desire to push its frontiers to the limits, is still very much a product of surrealism. Most contemporary poets and readers of poetry have learned from surrealism that poetry must ultimately "lead somewhere," that it is something other than a harmless confection of images and words, that it is intimately involved with and acts upon life. Surrealism expressed an ambition that has characterized almost all contemporary literature: to be more than literature. Its indictment of categories of society and of thought still determines our way of looking at things.

But the gap between surrealism and the most recent metamorphoses of literature continues to widen all the same. In the first place, surrealism, a movement of rebellion, was imbued with enthusiasm—enthusiasm for language itself, of which it was the first systematically free expression; and enthusiasm for the imagination, of which this language was the medium. Through the new juxtapositions of words (or of images in painting) it became intoxicated with a freedom that was sufficient unto itself. By contrast, the literature of the last twenty-five years, including poetry, has been conscious of the inadequate, precarious, and provisional nature of language and very much aware of the great distance separating language and life. It is an expression of rebellion, anguish, or criticism, without any compensating factor. Whether it takes the form of a cry of despair or a theoretical analysis, the literature of the present and the future would seem incapable of finding its consolation or its solution in the beauty of language.

The wane of surrealism had two major manifestations. First, some writers won a hold on the public after 1940 only by moving away from their surrealist beginnings. Paul Éluard (1895–1952, pseudonym of Eugène Grindel) and Louis Aragon (born 1897), for example, owed their popularity to their political commitment, to their poems inspired by the Resistance. Aragon has succeeded in remaining in the forefront because he has moved close to the most recent trends, such as that represented by the review *Tel Quel*.

A second manifestation of change is that the surrealists who occupy the highest place in the godless, demythologized pantheon of the literary consciousness of today are not André Breton (1896–1966) and not even Éluard or Aragon, but the dissident or banished surrealists, such as Antonin Artaud (1896–1948) and Georges Bataille (1897–1962). Breton never ceased to reproach Artaud and Bataille for inhabiting a world of hiatuses and anguish that he found unbearable; but his fundamental objection was that they had rejected lyricism. Despite new publications before his death in 1966, Breton became an isolated figure after the war, an historical monument, inasmuch as he continued to represent the original spirit of surrealism, seeking the "gold of the time" and believing he could capture it without assuming the commitments and suffering the poisoned anguish of historical time.

THE OLDER GENERATION
OF NOVELISTS

The post-1945 literary scene included many active writers who had begun their careers between 1925 and 1930. Their work still cannot be spoken of merely as historical fact, even though they no longer dominate contemporary literature. This group included Georges Bernanos (1888–1948), André Malraux (born 1901), Louis Aragon as a novelist, Henry de Montherlant (1896–1972), Marcel Jouhandeau (born 1888), Pierre Drieu la Rochelle (1893–1945), Antoine de Saint-Exupéry (1900–1944), Louis-Ferdinand Céline (1894–1961, pseudonym of Louis-Ferdinand Destouches), Jean Giono (1895–1970), Julien Green (born 1900), and Charles-Ferdinand Ramuz (1878–1947).

The essential contribution of these writers was through the novel—but novels that were among the first to provoke people to say, "This is no novel!" The end increasingly outweighed the means; invention, description, and the creation of characters were decidedly of secondary importance. Although these elements were used, they were strained and shamelessly subordinated to the basic purpose, which was to establish the author's relationship to the world, to capture, or rather to form, a way of looking at things and a style of living. The novel became for them a way of posing questions and answering them.

Hence the neglect of narrative, which was sometimes elliptical or condensed, sometimes discursive; hence the digressions and the irregularity of the flow, the stresses being placed according to internal resonance and not according to the logic of the events related; hence the unity —and often the monotony—of perspective and coloring. The world described was the world that fascinated the writer and formed his thought, not the outward diversity of the real world.

The differences among these writers was great, but for all of them the novel was first and foremost an essay on the self, a transmuted confession, an attempt to give concrete expression to a particular idea. It is not coincidental that, in addition to their novels, all these authors wrote essays. Bernanos wrote not only *Sous le soleil de Satan* (1926, Under the Sun of Satan) but also *La grande peur des bien-pensants* (1931, The Great Fear of the Orthodox); Malraux wrote not only *Les conquérants* (1928, The Conquerors), but also *La tentation de l'occident* (1926, The Temptation of the West); Montherlant wrote not only *Le songe* (1922, The Dream) but also *Service inutile* (1935, Useless Service); Giono wrote not only *Le chant du monde* (1934, The Song of the World) but also *Triomphe de la vie* (1942, Triumph of Life); Drieu la Rochelle wrote not only *Rêveuse bourgeoisie* (1938, Bemused Bourgeoisie) but also *L'Europe contre les patries* (1931, Europe against the Fatherlands); Saint-Exupéry wrote not only *Vol de nuit* (1931, Night Flight) but also *Terre des hommes* (1939, Man's Earth); Ramuz wrote not only *Jean-Luc persécuté* (1909, Jean-Luc Persecuted) but also *Besoin de grandeur* (1936, Need for Greatness); Jouhandeau wrote not only *Monsieur Godeau intime* (1926, Intimate Portrait of Monsieur Godeau) but also *De l'abjection* (1939, On Abjection) and *Essai sur moi-même* (1947, Essay about Myself). The regularity with which these writers alternated between fiction and expository prose can be found in no preceding generation of novelists.

When we think of their work, what springs to mind is not stories or characters, or even a narrative style, but a voice telling us of the values for which each lived. If anything grouped these writers together and defined them, it was undoubtedly their common ethical concern. They contrasted what was and what they were with what they wanted to be and do. In this connection Malraux once rightly spoke of a "Corneillian tradition." For Malraux, the value was heroism; for Saint-Exupéry, courage and duty; for Montherlant and Drieu la Rochelle, the quest for virility (through the adoption of a political stand where Drieu la Rochelle was concerned); for Aragon, social justice; for Ramuz and Giono, the naturalness of a certain way of life; for Bernanos, honor—Christian and French—and saintliness; and for Jouhandeau, the quest for salvation, sometimes in demoniac guise. They all tried to offer a key to life. Thus, their masters were not Valéry or Claudel or Gide or Marcel Proust (1871–1922), that is, not the writers who laid the foundations for a new narrative structure; instead, they seemed the descendants of François-René de Chateaubriand (1768–1848), of Maurice Barrès (1862–1923), of Charles Péguy (1873–1914), or in the case of Bernanos, of Léon Bloy (1846–1917).

The very fact that they used the novel more than they

served it, that they had no ambition to find a new basis for it, made them all the more inclined to abandon it if what they wished to convey could be more effectively put across by other means. In part, the invention and "dishonesty" of fiction alienated them from that genre that, by gift and training, they had initially chosen. This alienation also arose from a purely artistic crisis—a feeling that the novel had been surpassed in the creation of illusion by films, and even by television—and from their refusal or inability to join younger novelists in seeking new paths for fiction.

Unlike Malraux or Montherlant, Georges Bernanos possessed the traditional gifts of the novelist: an art of imagining events, an ability to compress time and still give a sense of its flow, and an ability to sympathize with characters very unlike himself. Bernanos's *Under the Sun of Satan* marked the debut of a true novelist; and *Journal d'un curé de campagne* (1936, The Diary of a Country Priest) showed his artistic maturity. But in the last ten years of his life he devoted himself almost entirely to political writings—to the articles collected in *Lettre aux Anglais* (1942, Letter to the English), *Écrits de combat* (1944, Combat Writings), *La France contre les robots* (1947, France against the Robots), *Le chemin de la Croix-des-âmes* (1948, The Croix-des-Âmes Road), and the posthumously published *Les enfants humiliés* (1949, The Humiliated Children).

Bernanos did not switch to the essay because he had run out of material for fiction. In 1934 he had written, "I had to wait until I was thirty-eight before I could start drawing on an inner experience that, as is sufficiently proved by my first book (if I may be forgiven for saying so myself), suffers from an excess of richness rather than poverty." His last novel, *Monsieur Ouine* (1943, Mr. Ouine), perhaps his masterpiece, was, if anything, overly rich; the unfinished novel *Un mauvais rêve* (1951, A Bad Dream) gives the same feeling; and his play *Dialogues des Carmélites* (1949, Dialogues of the Carmelites), which was also published posthumously, undoubtedly demonstrated that his inventive genius remained intact to the end.

Bernanos ceased to draw on this visionary world— although it continued magnificently to nourish his last works, despite the lack of finish and the lack of care— because of the pressing demands of the times, because of the need to combat, without any illusions, the trend toward decadence and disaster. And in spite of a narrative power much closer to such nineteenth-century writers as Dostoevski or Jules-Amédée Barbey d'Aurevilly (1808– 1889) than to his contemporaries, Bernanos's mistrust of fiction, which was shared outside of France at that time even by those who had most honored literature in general and the novel in particular (remember Thomas Mann's statement that the writer's major responsibility was not toward beauty, and Hermann Broch's rejection, through the character of Vergil in *Der Tod des Vergil*, of a work of art understood only as an aesthetic object), was one of the signs of Bernanos's modernity.

But his lapse into silence cannot be explained only by this mistrust of imaginative literature; a deeper motive brings him even closer to us. After *Mr. Ouine*, Bernanos was thinking of writing two more books: "After these two books, I shall have fulfilled my destiny. I shall have no more bread to offer the soul." How could political and polemical expression be the most nourishing bread, even if it is the most urgently needed? And how could his novels—which evoke the struggle of supernatural forces, show the way to salvation, and are concerned with the fate of each individual soul—be regarded as suspect and inessential? What happened was that Bernanos fell silent because he felt he had reached a point beyond which he could not go. The voice of the adult had gone as far as it was possible to go toward the unadulterated, original voice, the voice of childhood. But this primeval voice was finally unattainable; all that can be heard is a kind of whispering in front of a closed door. What is *said* reveals the contours of what will remain *unsaid*. Bernanos could say what he felt impelled to say only by going around it, by encircling it with one negative after another. ("Was it prayer? To tell the truth, she did not know and she would not have dared to describe this way what for her was but . . .".) Prayer, joy, and ecstasy can be described only in terms of what they are not.

The development of André Malraux was different from Bernanos's, although his abandonment of fiction was even more determined. Until 1940, Malraux was primarily a novelist; *The Temptation of the West* and a few shorter essays were much less important than the five novels that appeared over regular intervals: *The Conquerors* in 1928, *La voie royale* (1930, The Royal Way), *La condition humaine* (1933, The Human Condition), *Le temps du mépris* (1935, The Time of Contempt), and *L'espoir* (1937, Hope). Malraux originally intended *Les noyers de l'Altenburg* (1943, The Walnut Trees of Altenburg) as the first novel of a multiple-volume work, *La lutte avec l'ange* (The Struggle with the Angel), which he never completed.

After *The Walnut Trees of Altenburg* Malraux devoted himself to writings on the philosophy of art, of
which the most important were *Saturne* (1950, Saturn),
an essay on Goya; *Les voix du silence* (1951, The Voices
of Silence); *Le musée imaginaire de la sculpture mon-
diale* (1953–55, The Imaginary Museum of World Sculpture); and *La métamorphose des dieux* (1958, The Metamorphosis of the Gods). In 1967 Malraux published the
first volume of his *Antimémoires* (Anti-Memoirs), which
did contain a few fragments of narrative fiction. These
fragments, however, were all related to his old works—
to *The Walnut Trees of Altenburg* and to *The Royal
Way*. *Anti-Memoirs* was primarily a journal of his meet-
ings with Nehru, with Mao, of his conversations with
Charles de Gaulle. Malraux has announced a sequel to
Anti-Memoirs, but he does seem to have given up the
novel as an art form.

For Malraux, the novel was always based on a participation in history in the making. His characters only take
shape when they can live outside themselves and become
part of a movement that transcends them. To seek refuge
from the self in action is not to act for oneself but to
participate in an impersonal action. For the agnostic,
this transcendental energy has only one name—history.
Thus, in Malraux's novels the theme of revolution and
virile brotherhood (*The Human Condition*) alternates
with the theme of the solitary adventure (*The Royal
Way*).

But a time came, however—in 1940, to be precise—
when Malraux saw the vast flow of what until then he
had believed to be the goal of history crumble before his
eyes. At that point, he lit upon national solidarity, which
inspired the *Camp de Chartres* (Chartres Prisoners-of-

War Camp) sections of *The Walnut Trees of Altenburg*; later he would say, "I espoused the cause of France." Why then did he not write the epic of the French Resistance? It is as if the national myth were powerless to replace the revolutionary myth in his work. And, indeed, they were not comparable: the Resistance was not, and could not be, a movement of history, as revolution is for a Marxist or para-Marxist writer. In *The Walnut Trees of Altenburg* Malraux attempted to make up for this loss by abandoning history and seeking permanent human values; this is the theme of the intellectuals conversing beneath the arches of the monastery of Altenburg.

Malraux exalted permanent human values again in *The Voices of Silence*, in which the history of art played the role that political events had played in his novels. There was the same dispossession of the self for the sake of a transcendental energy; but unlike the situation in his novels, the history in *The Voices of Silence* has already been made, without Malraux's personal involvement in it. He could not find creative inspiration in this sort of history. And no doubt there would not have been an *Anti-Memoirs*, but instead a continuation of the unfinished *The Metamorphosis of the Gods*, if Malraux had not entered the lists again by acting as Charles de Gaulle's minister of culture for more than ten years.

Yet Malraux's experience in government was also powerless to give fresh impetus to his novel writing. As minister of culture, he participated in an administrative rather than an historic action. But even if he had been minister for foreign affairs or minister for Algerian affairs, the France of President de Gaulle was in any event no longer the kind of country that could direct history. What remained for Malraux was an evocation of the great men he encountered. But Nehru and Mao represented historical goals that were not his; and Charles de Gaulle, although an illustrious figure, belonged more to the past than to history in the making.

Malraux's gifts were not so much those of a novelist as those of an epic poet and reporter; nevertheless, his masterpiece is *Hope* and not *Anti-Memoirs*. For the resonance of a myth, which he needs, was lacking in *Anti-Memoirs* and was replaced by a rhetorical inflation that was even more marked in *Les chênes qu'on abat* (1971, Felled Oaks), an account of his last meeting with General de Gaulle, and in *Oraisons funèbres* (1971, Prayers for the Dead). Whereas the best parts of his novels were marked by a rapidity and an elliptical quality imposed by the richness and speed of the action, with the brilliance of the imagery and the rhetorical structure always present but merely hinted at, his later style has suffered from a kind of prolixity, an oratorical turgidness all too visibly punctuated by the same stylistic mannerisms. This oratorical inflation attempts to camouflage a literalness that the writer perhaps feels to be the lack of creativity; it is the mark of pangs of conscience in a reporter. Malraux has justified *Felled Oaks* as an interview by describing *The Human Condition* as reportage. But *The Human Condition* was a truly creative work and *Felled Oaks* is not good reportage, since General de Gaulle's actual words are blurred by the author's own paradoxically heightened style.

Examining his recent works, one can see why Malraux has won a wider public only by to some extent losing his original public. But the perspective of time will place in focus his best work, which, taken as a whole, was one of the most powerful achievements of twentieth-century

French literature. Although he may now seem somewhat remote from a literature that repudiates the myth of the hero and finds its truth in depreciation, or in the questioning and analysis of language, immediately after the war he appeared as the prophet of the troubled times and of commitment in literature.

When Aragon, long before he wrote *Les communistes* (1949–50, The Communists), was playing with words or dreams in works such as *Le Paysan de Paris* (1926, The Peasant of Paris), Malraux was writing *The Conquerors.* And Malraux's *The Human Condition*, published five years before Sartre's *La nausée* (1938, Nausea), was a metaphysical novel that brought us face to face with the absurd, the despair of lucidity, and the anguish of man's destiny. When Sartre, in *L'être et le néant* (1943, Being and Nothingness), said, "Man is the being who aspires to be God," he was echoing a phrase in *The Human Condition*: "Every man dreams of being God." Albert Camus (1913–1960), who was involved in a stage adaptation of Malraux's *The Time of Contempt*, also proclaimed his debt. And the example of Malraux's "novels"—which are not novels but something unclassifiable between reportage, epic, tragedy, and meditation—contributed to the disintegration of the novel, even though the subjects and themes of his works were in complete opposition to those of most postwar novels.

Two writers who did not survive the war bore witness both to the ethical inspiration of their generation and to the crisis of the novel, whose validity was already being questioned. Antoine de Saint-Exupéry, who disappeared while on a reconnaissance mission over occupied France in 1944, divided his literary work between reportage in the form of novellas—*Night Flight* and *Pilote de guerre*

(1942, Combat Pilot)—and reportage in the form of essays—*Man's Earth*. He was unwilling, and no doubt unable, to embark on a novel proper. His posthumously published *Citadelle* (1948, Citadel), a long allegorical tale, seemed to some to be closer to a novel; but in fact it was rather a philosophical tract. Saint-Exupéry's literary reputation, which has been very high in recent years and has spread beyond the borders of France, was enhanced by the heroism of his life and death. He was certainly not the great writer he has been thought to be, and people are beginning to realize this. Nevertheless, he was representative of his generation, not only because he accepted and lived to the full ethical values with which others merely played, but also because of some of his central preoccupations, particularly the idea of the *link* or *tie*, which prompted him to write, in *Un sens à la vie* (1956, A Sense of Life), that "man is no more than a knot of relationships" and that civilization "is concerned not with things but with the invisible ties that bind them together."

Pierre Drieu la Rochelle was also a victim of the war, but on the enemy side, so to speak: he committed suicide in 1945 after the collapse of the Nazis, whose cause he had espoused out of a misguided Europeanism. Drieu la Rochelle wrote intellectual problem novels and essays closely akin to confessions, but almost none of his books was able fully to contain his intriguing yet irritating mind —obsessed by the "immediacy of the twentieth century," grappling unhesitatingly with its demands, haunted by the problem of how to reconcile mind and body, seeking a life that would be an all-out risk and that would find its justification through its involvement in the collective destiny. His most successful work was his last, the post-humously published *Récit secret* (1958, Secret Account),

in which Drieu la Rochelle revealed his deep-seated sui-
cidal tendencies and showed how such intelligence and
such high demands could be transformed into impotent
anguish.

Henry de Montherlant—whom many, particularly
Bernanos, regarded as the major writer of his generation
—used both the essay and the novel to express his concept
of "wisdom," an art of living that consisted in following
the contradictory impulses of his nature through a principle of alternation, since he was unable to reconcile them:
the Christian versus the profane, the pagan, the stoic;
the taste for commitment, sacrifice, and austerity versus
the taste for sensuality, indulgence, and hedonism.

Montherlant's early novels, from *The Dream* in 1922
to the tetralogy *Les jeunes filles* (1936–39, The Girls),
all showed a remarkable and persuasive lightness of touch.
After 1942, from *La reine morte* (1942, Queen after
Death) through *Le cardinal d'Espagne* (1960, The Cardinal of Spain) and *La guerre civile* (1965, Civil War),
drama became his favorite means of expression. While
his plays served the same ethic and taught the same
lessons his novels did, Montherlant the dramatist was as
respectful of the traditional rules of drama as Montherlant
the novelist was free with those of the novel. This is why
his plays, despite their success, did not have the same
importance as his novels. He added nothing new to the
drama; instead, he took a content that remained the
same—and about which one could have many reservations—and arrayed it in fine, but outmoded costumes.
One exception was *La ville dont le prince est un enfant*
(1951, The City Whose Prince Is a Child); a play deeply
rooted in Montherlant's own knowledge of religious

schools and of adolescent passions, it had the seriousness of tragedy without its formal trappings.

Although Montherlant may have been overestimated at one time, his present fall from favor is equally unjust. In his later essays, such as those in *Va jouer avec cette poussière* (1966, Go Play with This Dust), which showed an astringent yet serene aloofness from the contemporary world, admirable touches often redeemed what could otherwise be trite and repetitious. Among Montherlant's other postwar works is the somewhat dated *La rose de sable* (1954, The Sand Rose), a late publication of a novel written before the war. But one of his most recent novels, *Le chaos et la nuit* (1963, Chaos and Night), may well be his masterpiece, even though it went almost unnoticed at the time of its publication. It told the story of the last days of a Spanish refugee, a survivor of the civil war, who has gradually become alienated from all his beliefs and acquaintances, and who decides to return to Spain although he knows that he will be a hunted man. He dies by an unknown hand in his hotel room, after attending a bullfight, which symbolically anticipates his murder. *Chaos and Night* is a complex, ambiguous, and very free work, in which we listen to the reflections of the author, become involved in the realistic illusion of the narrative, and at the same time meditate on the lesson of the enigmatic fable it relates.

Although Montherlant's *Un assassin est mon maître* (1970, A Murderer Is My Master) could not rival *Chaos and Night*, it was nonetheless a fine novel. It has recently been said that Montherlant's suicide "authenticated" his work, which can henceforth be seen only in the light of such an act.

The French-Swiss Charles-Ferdinand Ramuz was yet another writer caught between the novel and the essay. For him, truth meant harmony with nature, which surrounds and explains man.

Jean Giono has sometimes been compared with Ramuz, although their styles were completely different and nature in Giono's work was more the cosmos of a pagan epic. Giono's work showed considerable development after World War II. Before the war he used the novel as a vehicle for preaching. From 1947, when he returned to his literary career with *Un roi sans divertissement* (A King without Amusement) and *Noé* (Noah), he abandoned preaching for a kind of fiction that seemed to seek nothing beyond itself. And although in his problem novels he had been fairly free with the rules of the genre and used such forms as the folk tale and the epic, in his later fiction he reverted to more traditional forms, recapturing in *Le hussard sur le toit* (1951, The Horseman on the Roof), *Le bonheur fou* (1957, Mad Joy), and *Angelo* (1958, Angelo) the tone of Stendhal's (1783–1842, pseudonym of Marie-Henri Beyle) Italian chronicles.

These chronicles, in which Giono delighted in recapturing the distant past—for example, the Italy of the *carbonari*, duels, inns—did have a significance, but in a way quite unlike his earlier work. Giono's shift from commitment to escapism meant that he—a pacifist disoriented by the war—no longer believed in the possibility of living an authentic life in the modern world, even as an exception to the general rule. Gone was the embodiment of values in one's own existence, which obsessed his generation and which had obsessed him before the war. Giono no longer attempted to teach us how to live happily and freely; he wanted his writing to give the *feeling* of happiness and freedom. Happiness was not the happiness of Angelo on the roads of Italy but the happiness of Giono dreaming and writing about Angelo, and the happiness of his reader.

For Giono, existence became a void that could be filled only by playing with life, through words that play with life—through literature. One might think that this concern with language, which separated Giono from writers who, both in his generation and in the next, regarded it as a mere tool, would have found him disciples among those of the most recent literary trends. Yet those who now define literature as language above all have scarcely any interest in him. This is because for Giono language was a game: he accepted and took delight in language, and he was willing to make language conform to certain traditions (for example, the scope and tone of the chronicle); in more recent years, on the other hand, language has become the means for a joyless destruction.

The work of Louis Aragon has provided one of the most complex and original examples of the multiple possibilities of the novel and its place in literature. Initially, Aragon was in no way a novelist, even though his surrealistic imagery and arabesques of language found better expression in the partially narrative prose of *The Peasant of Paris* than in the poems of *Le mouvement perpétuel* (1925, Perpetual Motion). His definitive turn to the novel coincided with his becoming politically active. Adherence to communism dominated his "realistic" novels of the 1930s; *Les cloches de Bâle* (1933, The Bells of Basel) and *Les beaux quartiers* (1936, The Good Neighborhoods). Since Aragon wanted to contribute to

the emancipation of man and to work for the advent of
true social justice—and in so doing not only recount the
revolutionary legend but also (unlike Malraux) depict
the machinations and selfishness of bourgeois society—
he felt he had to use the most popular literary form and
to make it easily readable.

According to the dogma of socialist realism—and
Aragon's six-volume *The Communists* bordered on propaganda—the revolutionary novel had to follow the traditional novel form. Aragon's contribution to literature,
however, cannot be dismissed as that of a party-line militant. At the same time as these novels about the "real
world," he was writing his "scenes of private life." Works
such as *Les voyageurs de l'impériale* (1943, The Outside
Passengers), *Aurélien* (1944, Aurélien), and, even more
explicitly, *La mise à mort* (1965, The Death Blow) and
Blanche et l'oubli (1967, Blanche and Forgetfulness)
were full of autobiographical confessions, the confessions
of Aragon the lover, shot through with the myth he
created around his wife, Elsa. These confessions were
pursued in poetry—*Le roman inachevé* (1956, The Unfinished Novel), *Le fou d'Elsa* (1964, Elsa's Fool), *Les
chambres* (1969, The Rooms)—in which his verse closely
resembled the rhythms of prose, just as his prose has
often been a montage of poetic images.

Whether in prose or poetry, Aragon's work tries to
express and communicate something: first the surrealist
faith in imagination, then a political creed and the value
of love; and in his need to express, Aragon was a true
member of his generation. But his gifts and his self-
indulgent attitude toward language set him apart from
the others; whatever he was trying to say, it was the *way*

of saying it that he seemed to take most seriously.
Breton was more surrealistic than Aragon in *Nadja* (1928,
Nadja), Malraux more revolutionary in *The Human Condition*, Éluard more in love in *L'amour la poésie* (1929,
Love, Poetry). The surrealist myth and the communist
myth were attenuated in Aragon's work by the very brilliance of his writing, by the presence of the writer. Thus,
his surrealist poetry moved in the direction of a "modernist" fantasy akin to that of Giraudoux or Cocteau. And
his "committed" novels tended toward descriptions of
bourgeois settings: it was often difficult to distinguish
between his preoccupations with style—and with memories—and his polemical interest in the object described.

The war and the Resistance seemed to provide a solution for Aragon's basically tragic contradiction. There was
a happy marriage between the alexandrines of *Le crève-
coeur* (1941, Heartbreak) and of *La Diane française*
(1945, The French Diana) and a certain kind of nationalism, which, it is true, was also the nationalism of the
French literary tradition. And in a novel such as *La
semaine sainte* (1958, Holy Week), which depicted the
flight of Louis XVIII and the royalists during the Hundred Days as background to the story of the painter
Géricault, Aragon showed, because of the reminders of
the exodus of 1940 and of the withdrawal of the German
forces, a constant participation, although at one remove,
in the recent history of France. However, *Holy Week*
was a fairly traditional historical novel, but the alexandrine and rhyme, which Aragon not only used but justified in theory in *La rime en 1940* (1941, Rhyme in 1940),
were not easy to revive. The younger generation would
have nothing to do with any nationalistic, or even merely

historical, romanticism; and Aragon was too eager not to lose contact with contemporary literary movements. He was, moreover, sufficiently flexible and gifted, too gifted even, not to seek new paths.

He found them in his most recent novels (*The Death Blow* and *Blanche and Forgetfulness*), which were, above all—despite the confessional element and their political and moral significance—demonstrations of a temperament that strives to go beyond the individual and to conjure up the anonymous, mythical figure of the writer. "I never wrote my novels, I read them," he said recently in *Je n'ai jamais appris à écrire* (1969, I Never Learned to Write). Writing thus interpreted becomes impersonal dictation rather than a personal endeavor, and in this way Aragon has reconciled the surrealist automatic writing of his youth with the theories of a young generation he wishes to remain close to. And so, while most of his contemporaries are receding into the background, Aragon—not without some mental acrobatics—has succeeded in making his presence felt once again.

There are other gifted writers in the generation that began writing in the period between the two world wars. But their work showed no real development after World War II and is now rather remote from us.

Julien Green, whose last important novel, *Moïra* (Moïra), was published in 1950, has been devoting himself more and more to writing his memoirs. Unlike other major novelists of his generation, Green was never concerned with ethical humanism. His masterpieces—*Le voyageur sur la terre* (1927, The Pilgrim on Earth), *L'autre sommeil*, (1931, The Other Sleep)—expressed an anguish that links them more to the later existentialist novel and the novel of the absurd; Green's fictional world, created out of full-bodied, believable characters who usually live in the provinces, unfolded itself in traditional narrative forms. Green's religious conversion (rather than the evolution of the novel) seems to have paralyzed his creative impulse; hence his turning to the diary form.

Marcel Jouhandeau has continued to publish very regularly since World War II, but has added nothing essential to an enormous œuvre, whose strangeness and beauty are better appreciated in a collection of extracts. On the surface, Jouhandeau's universe is that of the nineteenth-century novel: stories of marriage, adultery, petty theft, and even crime take place in the imaginary village of Chaminadour, in the French provinces (it has been said that the provinces have provided the most fertile raw material for the French novel). Moreover, his style is classical, and he in no way puts language under attack. However, one feature of Jouhandeau's work links him with the contemporary novel: he has not put his fictional universe into a vast narrative cycle, as a nineteenth-century novelist would have done. Instead, he uses aphorisms, portraits, and meditations; or he merely collects the various banal incidences that could be the starting point for a sweeping epic. As a result, his novels are fragmented, and we have—like points of a graph that are not joined together—only the main indications of an experience, and reflections that he could have called, as he did one of his expository works, *Essay about Myself.*

Of all the writers of this generation, the one who has become most immediately relevant today is Louis-Ferdinand Céline, despite his temporary obscurity because of his anti-Semitic and anti-French attitudes, which made him an object of contempt during and after World War II. *Voyage au bout de la nuit* (1932, Journey to the End of the Night) was hailed as an event when it first appeared, but no 'one could then surmise the full extent of its influence. Going against the mainstream of the humanist, ethical literature of the day, it revealed a world without values, seen in all its nakedness. Céline was one of the first novelists to live what was to become the subject matter of literature—the absurdity of human existence. Moreover, the essential relationship between the absurd and the obscene—the obscene considered as a test of sincerity—would be found again in Georges Bataille, in Antonin Artaud, and in Jean-Paul Sartre. Indeed, Sartre's *Nausea* has a quotation from Céline on its title page.

Céline's influence was to make itself felt on style even more than on sensibility. It has been justly claimed that Céline's revolution was to substitute the spoken word for the written word. Yet Céline did not simply write the way people speak. His language—very highly wrought to achieve a sort of spontaneity or perpetual invention—took from the spoken language what went beyond the commonplace and the stereotype.

In Céline's alchemy of language slang is combined with metaphor and, particularly in *Journey to the End of the Night*, with cadences and breaks worthy of the symbolists. Sentences are often left unfinished; and trite, hackneyed phrases are replaced by exclamation marks or points of ellipsis. Was he attempting to destroy language in order to demonstrate its impotence, to say that there is nothing to be said, since everything is fake and nothingness? This is the interpretation of some of Céline's present-day admirers. Or was he attempting to destroy language in order to break its usual sequence, to set it on another course, and to make it capable of lending enchantment to pain and life to dreams?

A certain magic did mark *Journey to the End of the Night*, as well as *Mort à credit* (1936, Death on the Installment Plan), which, although less spontaneous and less lyrical, pushed the construction of a scatological fairyland even further. In his last works—*D'un château l'autre* (1957, Castle to Castle) and *Nord* (1960, North)—and in his posthumously published *Le Pont de Londres* (1964, London Bridge) and *Rigodon* (1969, Rigadoon), language (now the rhetoric of a counterrhetoric) was transformed into a kind of death rattle and was destroyed to no purpose. Language thus testified to the self-destruction of the author himself.

In his drive to self-destruction, Céline was constantly close to a literature that, like Artaud's work, suffered so much from its distance from life. However painful they might be, books like *Bagatelles pour un massacre* (1938, Bagatelles for a Massacre) and *L'école des cadavres* (1938, The School of Corpses) do not so much arouse disgust or disapproval as a harrowing sympathy for a man who was prey to obsessions of persecution and hatred and to prophecies of the end of the world. In some works, however, Céline did succeed in combining enchantment, scorn, and delirium in a totally original way. In *London Bridge* this magical Céline was present again, but not in *Castle to Castle*, an account of the tragicomedy of his collaboration with the Nazis, enmeshed in an historical truth that it cannot transmute.

"Céline points the way," Jean Dubuffet remarked. In any event, with Céline, the climate of postwar literature was already created.

FROM EXISTENTIALISM TO THE NOUVEAU ROMAN

During the first decade following World War II, French literature was dominated by the works of two writers who were very different from each other but who are linked under the label of *existentialism*. This label is an over-simplification, but it does point to similarities that cannot be ignored. These two writers—Jean-Paul Sartre and Albert Camus—together gave the novel a metaphysical rather than an ethical stress, and a new structure.

The most immediate and natural effect of the end of the war, however, was not the existential novel; it was a literature whose interest was not in its general vision of man but rather the specific historical events on which it fed; this literature sought to react spontaneously to the contemporary situation rather than to transform techniques. The underground literature of the war—the outstanding examples of which were the poems of Aragon and Éluard and the *récits* of Vercors (born 1902, pseudonym of Jean Bruller) (*Le silence de la mer* [1942, The Silence of the Sea] and *La marche à l'étoile* [1943, The

March toward the Star])—was followed, quite naturally, by a retrospective look at the Resistance. The best of these retrospective accounts were perhaps Roger Vailland's (1907–1965) *Drôe de jeu* (1945, A Strange Game) and Romain Gary's (born 1914) *Éducation européenne* (1945, A European Education).

The battles of the war provided the inspiration for *La vallée heureuse* (1946, The Happy Valley) by Jules Roy (born 1907) and *Week-end à Zuydcoote* (1949, Weekend at Dunkirk) by Robert Merle (born 1909). But the most important literature about the war was concerned with the world of the concentration camps. David Rousset's (born 1912) *L'univers concentrationnaire* (1946, The Concentration Camp Universe) was not a novel, since it was an attempt to give a structural description of the world of the camps; but it drew widely and powerfully on the narrative and descriptive techniques of the novel. In Robert Antelme's (born 1915) *L'espèce humaine* (1947, The Human Species), a deportee suffers his martyrdom without being able to reflect on its meaning, and a second character is able to do so by vicariously experiencing it through the other.

These years of captivity provided Jean Cayrol (born 1911) with the material for his trilogy *Je vivrai l'amour des autres* (1946–47, I Will Live the Love of Others). In this fictionalized account, the concentration camp, far from being an historical accident, becomes a symbol for man's earthly condition. Cayrol described this miserable, "Lazarus-like" condition in so uncompromising a way that he approached the world of Céline's outcasts and Samuel Beckett's tramps; but Cayrol interpreted this world exclusively in terms of religious redemption.

The most lasting literature of the immediate postwar years was not, however, these eye-witness accounts. It was a literature of thinkers, of philosophers—the writings of Sartre and Camus.

The first difference between Sartre and Camus and the group of "ethical novelists" who had come to the fore between the wars was naturally one of literary chronology. Although Sartre is almost the same age as Malraux, he began his literary career ten years later, with *Nausea* in 1938. His status as a writer was confirmed during the war years with the play *Les mouches* (1943, The Flies) and the treatise *Being and Nothingness*, and right after the Liberation with the first two novels of his trilogy *Les chemins de la liberté* (The Roads to Freedom): *L'âge de raison* (1945, The Age of Reason) and *Le sursis* (1945, The Reprieve). Camus began his career as a novelist in 1942 with *L'étranger* (The Stranger) and confirmed his importance during the late 1940s and early 1950s.

But this chronological gap between Sartre and Camus and the generation of Malraux and Bernanos was hardly the major difference. There were subtle but important differences in their thinking. Sartre and Camus, like the earlier writers, sought an ethic, which took the forms of freedom, commitment, and revolt; and both Malraux and Montherlant had already combined an ethical vision with a metaphysical conception of man, presenting the human condition as either tragically or serenely experienced. And it is not even altogether accurate to say that the interwar writers went from the ethical to the metaphysical while Sartre and Camus went from the metaphysical to the ethical; more precisely, the former merged what the latter were to separate.

The interwar writers, even if they were also essayists, reacted vitally and totally through the work of art; each book sprang from an *experience*, a moment, or a mood. The postwar writers were formal philosophers (Sartre) or thinkers (Camus), and the dialectic of their *thought* dictated the organization of their works, each one being a proposition or an experiment leading toward a conclusion. *Nausea* treated in isolation, or rather in abstraction, a pointless existence, just as *The Stranger* treated an absurd existence. *The Roads to Freedom* was above all concerned with a provisional solution to the problem of freedom; Camus's *La peste* (1947, The Plague) dealt in the same way with the problem of evil and revolt, and *La chute* (1956, The Fall) with the problem of guilt. Each of these works of fiction was constructed like a theoretical essay, its aim being to analyze fully a proposition.

Hence an important stylistic change. These writers would no longer let themselves be carried away by an impulse, would not arouse the emotions, would not seek to transmute experience. The aim was to be clear, accessible, simple. All earlier major novelists were to some extent poets. Sartre and Camus, although their prose styles were very different—Sartre discursive and familiar, Camus elliptic and aristocratic; Sartre closer to Émile Zola (1840–1902), Camus to Benjamin Constant (1767–1830)—were both prose writers who rejected the allurement of poetry (the only exception was a few lyrical essays Camus wrote as a young man during the late 1930s). Their writing was as antiromantic as their vision, tending sometimes toward what the critic Roland Barthes (born 1915) later called the "zero degree of writing," a mode of writing almost devoid of color, approaching the technique of naturalistic reporting (I myself once ventured to describe the literature they dominated as "metaphysical naturalism" rather than existentialism). Sartre was perfectly at home in the political polemics of the periodical *Les temps modernes,* as was Camus in the editorials he wrote for the newspaper *Combat.*

It was no accident that both Sartre and Camus regarded the theater as a more satisfactory means of expression than the novel, Sartre because he sought political effectiveness, and Camus no doubt because he was interested in the structure of tragedy and even in the staging of plays. But both of them probably favored the drama primarily because it uses a simpler language, which rejects overtones and avoids the superimposition of multiple voices and visions.

For insofar as he is the only one to think, the philosopher-novelist has to find some way of stilling his voice and effacing himself. The omniscient narrator, who, in the nineteenth-century novel, constantly intruded his point of view on that of his characters and commented on and announced events, did so only because he did not monopolize the thought: he was contradicted by his characters. But the uninvolved narrator, who stands outside, who adopts the point of view of his character without ever going beyond it, effaces himself only because his characters do *not* contradict him. When there is only one goal (the expression of truth itself), one voice is enough. The objective, neutral mode of writing guarantees the narrator's involvement in the character's situation, but also camouflages his own involvement. This mode of writing—in cinematic terms, *reduction of the visual field* —had already been used by Stendhal (unlike Balzac), by

the naturalistic novelists (Gustave Flaubert [1821–1881],
Maupassant), by some American novelists (Dos Passos,
Hemingway), and by Kafka. In stripping the narrative
of amalgams, additions, and subjective vibrations, these
men gave it maximum realism.

This concern for objectivity was undoubtedly all the
greater in the postwar philosopher-novelists because they
were so aware of their intellectuality. That is why they
pursued so insistently the process, already initiated, by
which the latent content of the novel, traditionally intermingled with its surface content, could rise to the surface
to occupy it entirely. More and more clearly, the characters, the plot, and the setting became only *media*; they
faded before a truth that could be a vision or merely an
idea (and which of the two it was determined whether
or not the work was successful).

In any event, there was an attempt (mainly by Sartre,
it is true, but Camus also wrote on the novel while the
earlier novelists never did) to formulate a dogmatic
aesthetic designed to provide the novel with a new and
durable basis. At the same time that *Nausea* appeared,
and in the same issue of the *Nouvelle revue française* that
contained an article by Sartre on phenomenology—which
was the manifesto of a philosophical realism, paying tribute to the philosopher Edmund Husserl for having given
us things, things in themselves, free from all idealistic
secretions—Sartre published an article entitled "M. François Mauriac et la liberté" (1939, François Mauriac and
Freedom). This article was the first of a series of studies
in which Sartre contrasted true and false practitioners of
the novelist's art. The false ones included Mauriac, Giraudoux, Giono, and Malraux, on whom Sartre an-

nounced a study that has yet to be published; the true novelists were Faulkner and Dos Passos.

Sartre's basic idea here was that the novelist cannot be both inside and outside at the same time. Either his field of vision is God's, who sees simultaneously the end and the beginning and who pierces through appearances (in which case he is explaining destiny, not portraying a life), or his field of vision coincides with the instant actually lived by someone, and his art is alive, encouraging a spontaneous response from the reader to the very freedom of the character. (Sartre was in fact wrong to make this law absolute, since Balzac's novels, which are undeniably full of vitality, used the same combination of perspectives as those of Mauriac. If this combination weakened Mauriac's novels, it is because perhaps the forms work only the first time and because, for historical reasons to be defined, another narrative perspective is needed.) In any event, this preliminary theorizing, which would be found (with different conclusions) in what ten years later was to be the *nouveau roman* (new novel), was one of the main differences between Sartre and his predecessors.

Literary reasons alone cannot account for the enormous success of Sartre between 1945 and 1955. He was not of the first rank as a novelist, a dramatist, a prose stylist, or even a philosopher, but he was nonetheless an outstanding writer because the range of his work was so broad and, more importantly, because he gave his contemporaries precisely what they needed. The disillusionment and despair arising from the horror of wartime events created a need for resolute thinking, for an orthodoxy that would face the world as it was, that would be alive to the world's problems, and that would not delude itself. People were attracted by the authority and systematic vigor in the contemporaneity and frankness of Sartre's thinking.

Nausea was a completely ahistorical metaphysical novel, whose success lay more in showing than in proving. Admittedly, Roquentin's interior monologues sometimes take the form of a meditation with a definable pattern and conclusions. The famous passage of the existential revelation, in the public park of Bouville, tells us explicitly that man is not essential to the universe, that he exists for no prearranged reason, that the world and himself are totally contingent ("contingent" in the philosophical meaning of neither logically necessary nor logically impossible). But we *feel* the nauseous disgust and the slack, heavy atmosphere of the novel much more than we follow the stages of a demonstration. The images, evoking the gratuitousness and "obscenity" of the physical world, and the writing itself, with its stricken, paralyzed quality, are more persuasive than any philosophy. But philosophy enters into the moral question that the book poses. On the last pages, the music of a record provides a gleam of the hope of salvation. The melody does not exist slackly and insipidly like man; it has a rigorous necessity. Perhaps man can follow its example and *be* rather than merely exist, by creating or living "perfect moments."

Shortly after *Nausea*, Sartre published a treatise significantly entitled *L'imaginaire* (1940, The Imaginary). Sartre promptly rejected this aesthetic temptation; but even in *Nausea* there was a separation between a visionary universe, which inspires a genuine artistic creation, and a philosophy seeking after values, which threatens the vitality of the novel and is likely to break away from it sooner or later. From *Nausea* to *The Roads to Freedom,* via *The Flies,* Sartre went from the entrapment of existence in the world to its liberation. Self-awareness is experienced as baseless, valueless. But if the nausea provoked by this recognition is overcome by admitting it honestly, this is enough to discover the "roads to freedom." Having no prearranged basis, man is his own basis; the fact that he is abandoned means that he is free. Freedom, finally, is the exalting, life-giving word (although proclaimed without the fervor attached to it by surrealism) that makes it possible to face up to the world. Life begins "on the other side of despair."

In a key scene in *The Flies* between Jupiter and Orestes, the freedom of man is contrasted with the order of the world; and the circumstances in which the play was written and performed—in Paris during the Nazi occupation —gave a clearly political connotation to a general philosophical concept. Echoing Orestes, Mathieu Delarue, the hero of *The Roads to Freedom,* decides to "accept responsibility for existence." All the characters in the trilogy thus live the experience of their freedom and are shown in their progress toward an unforeseeable future. Nothing weighs on them or forces them to be this rather than that—not God's commandments, moral imperatives, their past, their passions, their concept of themselves, or their social position. They are, to be sure, in a particular situation. But the situation determines nothing; it is no more than the setting for a choice or a decision. Does Mathieu love Marcelle? Will Marcelle keep the child? Does Daniel believe in God? Will Mathieu become a communist? Will he kill himself? Will Daniel kill the cats? The questions can only be settled by the acts that they will freely choose. And these acts allow of no hierarchy of alternatives: to commit oneself or not to commit oneself is to be equally free. Freedom is not an exceptional form of action; it is the common fabric of existence, to which we are all "condemned." This condemnation is the only value there is and it is called *responsibility*. Thus, "existentialism is a humanism," the only humanism that is consistent and free from illusion.

But this humanism of freedom raised a primary difficulty that threatened imaginative literature itself, insofar as the writer's experiential, obsessional world could be forced out by the thought that sets it free. A play like *Huis clos* (1945, Closed Door), an admirable evocation of the hell that for each of us is "other people," and also stories like *Intimité* (1939, Intimacy) and the best of *The Roads to Freedom*—for example, the scene in *The Reprieve* between the two sick people lying on their stretchers—conveyed the anguish and solitude, the impossibility of communication, and an eroticism deeper and stronger than any thought. The obsession with the original defilement and the horror of the viscous body fluids in which life has its origin block the movement leading to freedom and life. That is why Sartre, who drew his strength as a novelist from such obsessions, was to abandon the novel, since he wanted above all not to give expression to them.

Sartre was never to write the projected fourth volume of *The Roads to Freedom*. Instead, after the third part, *La mort dans l'âme* (1949, Sick at Heart), he abandoned the novel in favor of the theater, which is more suited to showing action than to evoking the climate of life, and which is a better vehicle for words of command. His skillfully written and very popular plays—*Les mains sales* (1948, Dirty Hands), *Le Diable et le bon Dieu* (1951,

The Devil & the Good Lord), *Nekrassov* (1955, Nekrassov), *Les séquestrés d'Altona* (1960, The Condemned of Altona)—had to confront another difficulty—the difficulty of the meaning that should be given to freedom itself.

At the very moment that Sartre the novelist was affirming the absoluteness and equivalent value of *all* freedom, Sartre the political thinker, in the manifesto launching *Les temps modernes* (October, 1945), was accusing bourgeois literature of having chosen the freedom of noncommitment: "The writer is *situated* in his age; every word has repercussions. Every silence too. I hold Flaubert and Goncourt responsible for the repression that followed the Commune because they did not write a line to prevent it. . . ." Taking the place of existentialism in Sartre's work, Marxism brought with it a hierarchy of freedoms and destroyed the mystique of humanism. What Sartre had taken for the metaphysical absurd became the social absurd. Hell was no longer the hostility of individual consciousness, but class inequality. Freedom was not a value, but a potential value that could be realized only after social alienation had been removed. Freedom for its own sake became freedom for a particular end; man the "futile passion" became effective passion.

In *Dirty Hands*, Hugo kills Hoederer on the orders of the party, thus giving his freedom a concrete meaning in line with the movement of history, but Sartre left the conclusion ambiguous, since perhaps Hugo also killed out of jealousy, and the party, changing its line, later disowns him. Sartre's subsequent plays left no room for subjective interpretations; they reflected the conviction that one must work for social emancipation and that this emancipation is to be achieved through collective action.

In *The Devil & the Good Lord*, Goetz, a German mercenary soldier fighting in the civil wars of the Reformation, arbitrarily chooses now good, now evil; and since he fails in either case, he shows the absurdity of all subjective morality. And in *The Condemned of Altona*, Frantz, the Nazi who isolates himself in his guilt, assuming responsibility for the history of his party and its action, ends in madness, because no one person can be solely responsible. But this is more a condemnation of subjectivity than a definition of objectivity. And the question remains as to what community one can put one's trust in.

For a time a hard-line communist, later the founder of a short-lived movement of the noncommunist left, then a communist once more, and today attracted by Maoism and the new left, director of the newspaper *La cause du peuple*, breaking and then renewing his ties with his friends at *Les temps modernes*—Sartre, although uncertain of his position, has in any event given up writing novels and plays, which he has condemned as ineffective, subjective, and in danger of being immediately taken over by the bourgeoisie (in this spirit he refused the Nobel Prize).

Nevertheless, Sartre still writes—and writes well—almost as if to say that his farewell to literature is delayed by a weakness that postpones the substitution of action for words. *Critique de la raison dialectique* (1960, Critique of Dialectical Reason) opened the paths of historical pragmatism to philosophy. *Les Mots* (1964, The Words) analyzed, without self-indulgence, his literary vocation. In it Sartre accused himself of being interested only in words, his own and those of others; but he made these accusations in a style new to him: sharp, lively, brilliant, almost the style of Voltaire (1694–1778, pseudonym of François-Marie Arouet)—one that we sense he took great pleasure in.

L'idiot de la famille (1971, The Idiot of the Family) was a monumental study of Flaubert (the 2000 pages of the first two volumes are only a beginning). In "settling accounts" with the man who for a long time has been in his eyes the very model of the writer, he is also settling accounts with literature itself and putting an end to a long fascination. Sartre said that he will continue the book only because he has begun it and that he will write no more afterward. Nevertheless, *The Idiot of the Family* objectively represents a beginning, although it may subjectively represent a farewell. It is a model of how to integrate Marxist criticism and psychoanalytical criticism, an attempt at real understanding of its subject, at totalization as opposed to the open grillwork of structuralist criticism. It is also a portrait that is constantly being erased and redrawn in the process, one that remains a quest to the very end.

Sartre clearly still has much more to offer. But the exigencies and the scruples of a moral, not to say religious, conscience, which has made Sartre unwilling to share with some what cannot be grasped by all, has made him suppress—at least in part—the richness of his artistic and philosophical mind.

And yet, when Sartre proclaimed in the opening manifesto of *Les temps modernes*, "We do not want to be ashamed of writing, and we have no wish to talk in order to say nothing," he had hoped to impose his mark on a whole age of literature by presenting a doctrine, a commitment to the present, and an aesthetic theory of the novel. He had secured the collaboration of the best writers for his journal: Malraux himself (the first suggested title for the journal was *La condition humaine*), Camus, Raymond Queneau (born 1903), Michel Leiris (born 1901), as well as the sociological observer Raymond Aron (born 1905), and Maurice Merleau-Ponty, (1908–1961), the most rigorous of philosophers. Political differences soon broke up the team, but there were literary differences, too. Today *Les temps modernes* has become a sociopolitical review.

But Sartre's influence on fiction in the ten years after the war was substantial. There was an "existentialist," even a specifically Sartrian flavor in many novels, above all in those of Simone de Beauvoir (born 1908). Her first novel, *L'invitée* (1943, The Invited Woman), remains her masterpiece. Her subsequent novels, *Le sang des autres* (1944, The Blood of Others), *Tous les hommes sont mortels* (1947, All Men Are Mortal), and *Les Mandarins* (1954, The Mandarins), in all of which one can see the influence of both Sartre and Camus, were weakened by a too-obvious didacticism. But Beauvoir abandoned fiction fairly soon to write essays (*Le deuxième sexe* [1949, The Second Sex]) and memoirs (*Mémoires d'une jeune fille rangée* [1958, Memoirs of a Dutiful Daughter], *La force de l'âge* [1960, The Prime of Life], *La vieillesse* [1970, Old Age]), in all of which she neglected no opportunity to denounce the bourgeoisie.

The novels of Raymond Guérin (1905–1954)—*Quand vient la fin* (1941, When the End Comes), *L'apprenti* (1946, The Apprentice), *Les poulpes* (1953, The Octopi) —pitiless and bitter indictments of the absurdity of existence, can be compared with *Nausea*. But they completely lacked any spirit of positive humanism. Violette Leduc (1907–1972) can also be grouped with the existentialists. Her first essay, *L'asphyxie* (1946, Asphyxiation), was published by Camus. Her novel *La bâtarde* (1964, The Bastard), prefaced by Simone de Beauvoir, more a "scandalous" autobiography than a novel, was both deliberately frank and revolutionary in its social implications.

In the work of Henri Calet (1903–1955) one can find, together with a restrained pathos, the same refusal to compromise, the same iconoclasm, and the same determination to conceal nothing. Both Calet's *La belle lurette* (1935, Ages Ago) and René Etiemble's (born 1909) *L'enfant de choeur* (1937, The Choir Boy) were significant precursors of postwar fiction.

The works of Boris Vian (1920–1959)—such as *L'écume des jours* (1947, The Scum of Days), which showed the influence of Sartre—belonged to the folklore atmosphere of the liberation and the existentialism of the cellars of Saint-Germain-des-Prés. Vian's refusal to make any commitment, his poetic handling of language, and the melancholy of an adolescent inspiration won him a special place in contemporary literature, despite his premature death.

Among other existentialist novelists, one could also mention Marcel Mouloudji (born 1922) and Colette Audry (born 1906). But apart from Sartre, the existentialist novel produced only one writer of the first rank—Albert Camus.

The progression of Camus's career was very close to Sartre's. Taking a metaphysical realization as his starting point, he sought an ethic and a commitment. *The Stranger* corresponds to *Nausea*; Camus's concept of the absurd was not far from Sartre's notion of contingency. The "sensibility of the absurd that can be found scattered through the century" (as Camus stated in *Le mythe de Sisyphe* [1942, The Myth of Sisyphus], which set out to analyze the absurd philosophically) was embodied in *The Stranger*.

Meursault, the protagonist of *The Stranger*, to whose field of vision the narrative is restricted, is, like each and every one of us, absurd man; although he wants to find a justification for existence, he cannot. The feeling of the absurd derives from the conflict caused when objective reality thwarts our subjective desire for a valid life in a rational universe. So we become indifferent, we become strangers to ourselves. Meursault, however, does not destroy himself but allows himself to live; but in so doing, he allows himself to be condemned to death. How have we the courage to live in this absurd world? In *The Myth of Sisyphus* Camus replied that life, an ethical life, is both bearable and viable, provided that the truth of the absurd is accepted and provided that all escapes—suicide, religious faith, and hope—are rejected. The one indispensable value that makes life possible is mental lucidity.

Thus, at its worst, life is still bearable; the absurd is not all-pervading. "The absurd is inconsistent with existence. It excludes value judgments, but value judgments do exist. They exist because they are linked with the very fact of existence," Camus wrote in an essay, *Remarque sur la révolte* (1945, A Note on Revolt), a few years after *The Myth of Sisyphus*. By living and acting, man's existence takes on meaning, which is crystallized by one experience in particular—rebellion. Rebellion proves that we are not prepared to accept the unacceptable, that we cannot just let things happen, and that there are things worth defending. And what is worth defending is not the individual alone, but mankind. "The individual is not, in himself, the embodiment of the values he espouses and defends. Humanity, taken as a whole, embodies these values. When a man rebels, he identifies himself with other men."

The Plague embodied the transcending of the absurd. And it is significant that this book was simultaneously an allegory of the eternal human condition and a chronicle of the recent past. One can recognize in the city of Oran —fallen prey to the plague, shut in by its own tragedy, but calling for devotion and sacrifice—France during the Nazi occupation. And indeed, it was in the Resistance that Camus himself demonstrated, and lived to the full, values that cannot be reduced to the absurd. In *The Plague* the values that come to the fore are caring for others, understanding, and limiting the spread of evil. There is a kind of prudence here that limits the meaning of commitment and contrasts it with the Sartrian choice.

In *L'homme révolté* (1951, The Rebel) Camus clearly establishes the theoretical basis of these themes. The ethic born of the rebellion against evil rediscovers the obsession with evil by questioning its own consequences. How can we ensure that a new evil will not arise from our actions? Given certain events (the disillusionment after the liberation of France, the degradation of the revolutionary spirit by the dictatorships in the Soviet Union and in the "people's democratic republics"), Camus was haunted by the fear of the evil that can stem from action in the service of good. He denounced the forms modern rebellion has taken, and he condemned the Marxist and Hegelian religion of history, at the risk of cornering himself into a passive ethic of nonintervention, understanding, and charity.

The path Camus followed in his plays paralleled that of his novels and essays. Just as the lyricial monologue of *Caligula* (1938, Caligula) corresponded to his first essays, *Le malentendu* (1944, The Misunderstanding)—a somewhat melodramatic play in which a man is murdered by his mother and sister, who fail to recognize him—was an extension of *The Stranger*. *L'état de siège* (1948, State of Siege) took up again the theme of *The Plague*. And *Les Justes* (1949, The Just), which portrayed Russian terrorists as "sensitive murderers," tormented by the contradiction between the end and the means, was linked to *The Rebel*. After *The Just* Camus abandoned the theater, disillusioned by a failure that contrasted with the success of his novels, although his plays were no more unconventional in technique than Sartre's.

In *The Fall*, a novel that is a long monologue by a single character, Camus attempted to transcend his previous work. The hero, an apparently decent man, one day perceives the hypocrisy of his virtues, accuses himself, and becomes both judge and penitent. Thus, good conscience, subjective morality, and minimum intervention, with which Camus had appeared to be satisfied, are deprived of their mystique. But how can the will to act for the common good be reconciled with the need to accept final responsibility for such action oneself and prevent it from being deflected and despoiled by history? Cut short by his early death, Camus's work remained inconclusive. But would the situation have been otherwise had he lived? Camus would doubtless have tried to seek a conclusion without returning to inner complacency, but without ever accepting Sartre's delegation of responsibility—on the contrary, his work would have become a dialogue between positive and negative arguments. In this unstable equilibrium, in the "agonized serenity" (to quote an expression of a poet he loved, René Char [born 1907]) of those moments in which contradictions seem about to be resolved, the genius of Camus would have found the subject matter of other narratives. The rhythm of his last works, such as *L'exil et le royaume* (1957, Exile and the Kingdom), attempts to reassemble and restore the unique contrary throb of life. And it is a rhythm of poetry.

Unlike Sartre, Camus was first and foremost an artist, a man who had faith in art. He did not go along with the tendency to despise language or to question its validity. In this he resembled the great writers of the early twentieth century (Gide in particular); he strove to combine the values of a new sensibility with traditional language, which he handled with mastery and brillance. He reduced the force of language in *The Stranger* through the objectivity of the writing, but he gave language free rein not only in the lyricism of his early essays but also in the tense and insistent rhythm of *The Fall*.

Camus did not have Sartre's vigor and originality as a philosopher, and certain passages of *The Rebel* come perilously near the scholarly dissertation. He was also incapable of creating the obsessional universe that gave the work of Sartre its creative power. The poverty of Camus's fictional imagination was evident. A few banal events, which reappeared from one book to the next, served merely as a pretext (the subject of *The Misunderstanding* was announced in *The Stranger*, and *The Plague* is related to the subject of *The Stranger*). Furthermore, his characters have no real life: Meursault and Caligula are myths, and both Rieux and Tarrou in *The Plague* are simply mouthpieces of the author. *The Stranger* is more a long story than a novel; *The Plague* is an allegorical chronicle, halfway between Anatole France (1844–1924, pseudonym of Anatole-François Thibault) and Kafka; *The Fall* is a mythic monologue. But though Camus was not a great novelist, he was a great writer, a thorough-bred writer, who put his art at the service of reflecting the perplexities of his time.

Although existentialism dominated fiction from 1945 to 1955, the novel appeared under other banners as well during this period. In the first place, the traditional novel continued to be written, and though the writers who perpetuated it could not help modifying it in light of new values, such modifications did not affect its essential character. For them the novel's manifest content (plot, characters, geographical and social setting) remained as important as its latent content (the author's own purposes and preoccupations). Whether or not this latent content was present determined whether a particular novel was a creative work or merely a potboiler. There is no point in listing here novels in which the author merely applied a well-tried technique to a carefully chosen subject, if such novels were lacking in any originality or effort. Such novels often became best-sellers, since the general public—despite the availability of movies and television—has retained an appetite for novels of entertainment, although its choice tends to light on a small number of works. Most such best-sellers are, however, quickly forgotten.

But there are exceptions, one of the prime ones being the novels of Georges Simenon (born 1903). If there is some justification in asking whether Simenon is not, after all, one of the great names of contemporary literature, it is not because of those of his works that have pretensions to literature—*Pedigree* (1948, Pedigree), in particular— since they are not among his best, but because of his monumental series of detective novels, especially those concerning Inspector Maigret. Undoubtedly, the assembly-line rhythm of his output, the tireless repetition of the same basic pattern, and the economy of his writing— in spite of its limited goal it never lapses into vulgarity— are all signs of paraliterature. But it is hard to deny some kind of genius to such imaginative richness. Simenon's ability to conjure up a scene is unparalleled, a great gift, however it may be used. And, more importantly, Simenon's fictional world is governed by a specific set of obsessions and sensations—whose recurrence is significant and not merely mechanical—and by a vision of man, his solitude and emptiness. It belongs to the vision of contemporary literature without being indebted to it in any way. Gide regarded Simenon as the greatest living novelist, and one is sometimes tempted to agree with him.

Among other writers who did not challenge the traditions of the novel, one of the best has been Louis Guilloux (born 1899), whose *Le sang noir* (1935, Black Blood) was one of the finest books of the interwar period, its achievement falling between Malraux's *The Human Condition* and Céline's *Journey to the End of the Night*. *Le jeu de patience* (1949, The Game of Patience), the story of a little Breton town during the occupation, reaffirmed Guilloux's exceptional gifts as a storyteller.

Marcel Arland (born 1899), whose *L'ordre* (1929, Order) has been awarded the Prix Goncourt, continued after the war to add to his substantial œuvre. Arland has combined his interest in philosophy (which he taught) with a stylistic grace and a skill in handling dialogue and narration. His postwar works have included *Il faut de tout pour faire un monde* (1947, You Need a Little of Everything to Make a World), *L'eau et le feu* (1956, Water and Fire), *Le grand pardon* (1965, The Great Pardon), and *Attendez l'aube* (1969, Wait for the Dawn).

Other worthy traditional novelists of the immediate postwar period—all of whom began writing before the Liberation—were Henri Bosco (born 1888) (*Le mas Théotime* [1946, The Théotime Farm], *Malicroix* [1948, Malicroix]); Marguerite Yourcenar (born 1903, pseudonym of Marguerite de Crayencour) (*Mémoires d'Hadrien* [1951, Memoirs of Hadrian], *L'œuvre au noir* [1969, A Study in Black]); and Paul Gadenne (1918–1956) (*Siloé* [1941, Siloam], *L'invitation chez les Stirl* [1955, The Invitation to the Stirl Home]).

Among those who started writing after 1945, particularly noteworthy has been Pierre Gascar (born 1916), whose novels—such as *Les meubles* (1949, Furniture) and *Le temps des morts* (1953, The Season of the Dead) —with their heavy obsessional atmosphere, have shown some of the characteristics of existentialism. Other traditionalists have included José Cabanis (born 1922), who transformed nostalgic confessions into subtle tales in such works as *Le bonheur du jour* (1960, The Day's Happiness) and *Les jeux de la nuit* (1964, Night Games); Françoise Mallet-Joris (born 1930), whose best novel perhaps remains *Le rempart des béguines* (1951, The Rampart of the Béguines); and Michel Mohrt (born 1913), whose first important novel, *Mon royaume pour un cheval* (1949, My Kingdom for a Horse), depicted the political confusion caused by the war, and whose latest books, in particular *La prison maritime* (1961,

Maritime Prison), skillfully played with new techniques while filling the writer's basic need to tell a story and create individual characters.

Affected by contemporary events, but reacting against the existentialist novel, against its criticisms of society and of language, against its pessimism and its philosophical seriousness, was a group of young writers around 1950 whose masters were Paul Morand, Jacques Chardonne (1884–1968) and Marcel Aymé (1902–1967). These novelists were for the most part politically conservative, ill at ease in the atmosphere of France after the Liberaation, skeptical about any progressivist ideology, and eager to please, to write well, and also to shock.

Jacques Laurent (born 1919), who as Cécil Saint-Laurent wrote the enormously popular novel *Caroline chérie* (1947, Caroline Darling), ridiculed Sartre in polemical essays, attacking his problem novels and the ponderousness of his Germanic philosophy. Antoine Blondin (born 1922) showed brilliant verve in *L'Europe buissonnière* (1949, Truant Europe). And Roger Nimier (1925–1962) wrote charming yet irritating, individualistic novels: *Les épées* (1949, The Swords), *Le hussard bleu* (1950, The Blue Horseman). These three writers have been the most significant representatives of a neoclassical group, which still exists in a way but which failed to form a genuine school as an alternative to existentialism and the *nouveau roman*.

More spontaneous, and without any theoretical or political afterthought, have been the novels of Françoise Sagan (pseudonym of Françoise Quoirez, born 1935), including *Bonjour tristesse* (1954, Hello Sadness) and *Un certain sourire* (1956, A Certain Smile). Sagan has been related to the neoclassical school by her style and even more by her desire to speak for a young generation which became conscious of itself only after the war and which reacted against its elders with a lucidity that was both frivolous and despairing.

The work of André Dhôtel (born 1900) lies somewhere between the traditional and the poetic novel. His primary goals have been to tell a story, to create characters (especially groups and families) and to describe the settings of villages and small towns in the Île de France, Champagne, and Ardennes regions. The exactness and subtlety of his art as a storyteller is, however, combined with a mysterious and fascinating poetic quality. *Les rues dans l'aurore* (1945, The Streets at Dawn) was perhaps Dhôtel's masterpiece. But *Les chemins du long voyage* (1949, The Roads of the Long Journey), *L'homme de la scierie* (1950, The Man from the Sawmill), and *Le mont Damion* (1964, Mount Damion) have all added increasing force to the work of a writer who has depicted a universe that is simultaneously realistic and mythical.

Unaffected by any events, currents, or countercurrents of contemporary life, novelists much more uncompromisingly poetic than Dhôtel extended and developed the attitudes and techniques of the surrealists into the postwar period. The underrated writer Georges Limbour (1901–1970) was typical of this group. He began his career in the interwar period by publishing works in various genres: *Soleils bas* (1924, Low Suns), which Cocteau and Aragon hailed as one of the finest poems of the day; the short stories of *L'illustre cheval blanc* (1930, The Illustrious White Horse); and the novel *Les vanilliers* (1938, The Vanilla Plants), which was his masterpiece. Although Limbour had been a member of the surrealist movement, he pursued a completely independent path after the war. He created a somber world of very private fantasy in such works as *Le bridge de Madame Lyane* (1948, Madame Lyane's Bridge), *La chasse au mérou* (1953, The Quest for Rockfish), and the play *Elocoquente* (1967, Elocoquente). Limbour had little interest either in literary fashion or public taste.

Limbour's is a variegated, enchanted world, ingenuous and melancholy, in which the adult nostalgically captures and delicately toys with the beautiful dreams of childhood. His stories are myths rather than anecdotes; there is not a single detail that is not governed by the special relationship between the poet and the universe. But the details are always images; his world is in no way an abstract allegory, but a succession of tastes, colors, sounds, and smells. His stories are imbued with a singularly appealing sense of fantasy; they are myths recounting the harmony of animate beings and objects in the green paradise of childhood, in the happiness of a sensuality devoid of sin. His books have the brilliance and also the evanescence of a last display of fireworks, and they are sustained by an admirable use of poetic language: learnedly rhetorical, yet delicately graceful.

André Pieyre de Mandiargues (born 1909), a few years younger than Limbour, participated in the last metamorphoses of the surrealist movement and, like Limbour, he has been passionately interested in painting. But Pieyre de Mandiargues made his literary debut many years later than did Limbour. He began by publishing stories that revealed a very individualized romantic surrealism such as those in *Dans les années sordides* (1943, In the Sordid Years), *Le musée noir* (1946, Black Museum), and *Soleil des loups* (1951, The Wolves' Sun). In recent

years he has won a much wider public (he was awarded
the Prix Goncourt in 1967) by moving much closer to
the dimensions and even the laws of the novel in *Le lis
de mer* (1957, The Sea Lily), *La motocyclette* (1963,
The Motorcycle), and *La marge* (1967, The Margin).
But his universe has remained very much the same, although the part played by eroticism has become increasingly important. His is a world of the unusual, even of
the extraordinary, but placed in a realistic setting that
excludes fantasy and any suggestion of a transcendental
surreality. In this world the unusual lacks magic; the
unusual does not pierce the veil obscuring what lies beyond it, but is rather marked by a somewhat decadent
aestheticism.

What Pieyre de Mandiargues discovers in the universe
always resembles what a collector of antiques with more
intuition than most people discovers in an antique shop
—a precious trinket that has gone unnoticed. His sense
of the extraordinary has an aristocratic tinge: it is the
self-indulgence of a superficial imagination that has no
need to enlarge its scope. And Pieyre de Mandiargues's
eroticism is of the same order; it is not the delirium it
can be, but a perverse, refined game. Yet his art does have
originality and value because, shallow though it may be,
it is troubling and disturbing. The reader is always on
the verge of falling into a strange perplexity. But the
style itself saves the reader from such disorientation. He
is always aware of an exquisite, delicate, and controlled
mode of writing, in which the length and fragility of the
sentences—with their pauses, hesitations, and digressions
—balance the rigorous forward movement of the book.

Among other writers who have contributed to the postwar poetic novel, Yves Régnier (born 1914), who attracted attention for *Le royaume de Bénou* (1957, The Kingdom of Bénou), moved toward the "novel of speech" of Maurice Blanchot and Louis-René Des Forêts (born 1918) in *La barette* (1967, The Biretta). But Régnier has rejected the abstractness of Blanchot and Des Forêts. Marcel Schneider (born 1913) found inspiration in German romanticism for *Le granit et l'absence* (1947, Granite and Abscence) and *Le chasseur vert* (1950, The Green Huntsman). Noël Devaulx (born 1905), whose first stories, those in *L'auberge Parpillon* (1945, The Parpillon Inn), were discovered and introduced to the public by critic Jean Paulhan (1884–1968), has not found the audience he deserves. Serious, rigorous, sometimes fairy-tale-like, but never superfluous, Devaulx's work is an obsessive questioning, a fantasia of death.

But the most important contemporary practitioner of the poetic novel has undoubtedly been Julien Gracq (born 1910). Gracq, who declared his debt to André Breton by publishing an essay on him in 1948, started writing in 1938, the year Sartre's *Nausea* was published, with the novel *Au château d'Argol* (The Castle of Argol). Bordering on the gothic novel, it attested to the continuing effectiveness of the imaginary and the irrational. The novels that followed, *Un beau ténébreux* (1945, A Dark Stranger) and *Le rivage des Syrtes* (1951, The Banks of the Syrtes), showed a preoccupation with mythology and imagery comparable to that of the romantic and surrealist poets. But the descriptions, the analyses, and the dialogue were handled with the skill of a genuine novelist and also with a flair for the dramatic. (Gracq, incidentally, tried writing for the theater with *Le roi pêcheur* [1948, The Fisher King].)

A *Dark Stranger* and *The Banks of the Syrtes* are dramatic novels because their subject is the intrusion of conflict into lives of people who believed themselves to be safe from it. Allan, the dark stranger, appears, and the daily routine is transformed into destiny, with everyone overwhelmed by "this rising tempest"; Aldo, a patrician youth, arrives on the banks of the Syrtes, and the war between the realms of Orsenna and Farghestan, which had been dormant for three centuries, bursts forth anew. Allan will die; Orsenna will be destroyed. Yet the drama in both novels is kept at a distance, like an image always sought after but never really attained. Behind the surface story, told in a very precise descriptive style, is an implicit story, a myth. Each character, each place, and each scene is presented not so much for its own sake as to represent magic forces or realities which we sense around us but which the analytical voice of reason cannot name. And the enchantment of these novels is both sustained and reinforced by a highly wrought and brilliant style. The sentence structure, eloquent and serene, is also powerfully dramatic, yet has a surface calm.

Gracq's most recent novel, *Un balon en forêt* (1958, Balcony in the Forest) set in the war year of 1940, brought fable closer to contemporary reality. The same is true of two of the three stories collected under the title *La presqu'île* (1970, The Peninsula). One takes place at the end of World War I. The second is simply a story of a man waiting for a woman; while Gracq analyzes his wait, he gives the detailed description of places that are easily identifiable, although the names have been altered. Has Gracq rejected his surrealist past? Does he now think that the real is richer than the imaginary? Perhaps. But we must not forget that the surrealist imagination also focused on the everyday world. Gracq's descriptions, however precise, are nonetheless suffused with imagination and are a far cry from the realistic reporting of today. Reality itself—historical or geographical reality—now seems mysteriously oriented, strangely burning beneath the ice of factuality.

Several writers of this same generation, who were related (at first, closely related) to the existentialist movement, moved away from it to pursue a much freer form of fiction, with a greater importance given to the play of language itself. And they demanded more from language than the lyrical seductiveness of the work of a writer like Julien Gracq. The influence of these writers, at first obscured by the vogue of Sartre and Camus, has not ceased to grow.

Raymond Queneau was connected with the surrealist movement from 1924 to 1929. For a time he was a contributor to Sartre's *Les temps modernes*, and his poems and songs—those in *Si tu t'imagines* (1951, If You Imagine)—were tinged with the existentialist folklore of Saint-Germain-des-Prés. Queneau's first novel, *Le chiendent* (1933, A Fly in the Ointment), presented a desertlike vision of the world, not far from Sartre's contingency and Camus's absurd. But this vision was presented indirectly, from the angle of ironic fantasy. And one can find in the character Saturnin's slangy monologue a prophetic caricature of existentialism. The most striking thing about *A Fly in the Ointment* was the verve, the freedom, and the comicality of the language; the book was a vast play on words, and Queneau's master was clearly James Joyce. Queneau freely mingled slang with the standard language; he wrote as people spoke. (Indeed, linguists will find in his works an invaluable source of information on the varieties of language, even of spelling.)

In *Pierrot mon ami* (1942, Pierrot, My Friend), although the dialogue was still based on spoken language, the brawl at the beginning is recounted in the manner of the Iliad. In *Les temps mêlés* (1941, Mixed Rhythms) Queneau told a story in three different forms (poetry, fiction, and drama). And in *Exercices de style* (1947, Exercises in Style) he presented the same absolutely insignificant incident (a quarrel in a Parisian bus) in ninety-nine versions, each one differing in syntactic structure, verb tense, figures of speech, and so on.

This emphasis on verbal content indicates that, for Queneau, language has been more than a means of expression; it is the essential reality of an œuvre that has always highlighted the play of language, an œuvre that is a continual "exercise in style." This is why Queneau has been so influential, even though his attitude toward language is very personal and cannot be reduced either to the liberating effusions of surrealism or to the more recent attacks on all set forms of expression. Note should be taken of Queneau's extraordinary juxtaposition of the crudest of colloquial styles and formal rhetoric. His approach to rhetoric is neither mere parody nor mere inventory; it is both a kind of nostalgia for the language of the past and an appeal for a viable contemporary language. Queneau's care in giving most of his poems a fixed form (ballad, ode) should not be interpreted as fidelity to ancient rhetoric, or as a satire on rhetoric itself, but rather as an appeal for a new rhetoric. Neither an accepter nor a destroyer of language, Queneau has sought a rejuvenation of the literary language, perhaps even a new classicism.

But Queneau is a spinner of dreams as well as words. The form and not the subject may be all-important, but there are images and situations to which he has constantly returned. For example, although *Pierrot, My Friend* (a parody of a detective story, in which it is not certain that the crime has been committed) was a novel whose subject is language itself, *Loin de Rueil* (1945, Far from Rueil) was clearly a novel of content, of dreams whose vehicle is language. Queneau has created a world of his own—a world that is out of step and somewhat clandestine—and not only in *Far from Rueil* but also in *Le dimanche de la vie* (1952, The Sunday of Life), *Zazie dans le métro* (1959, Zazie in the Subway), and *Les fleurs bleues* (1965, The Blue Flowers). This world is both the present-day world and a world of madness; a world of caricature and of poetry; a world of neighborhood theaters, empty lots, slot machines, fairgrounds, trains, and subways; an everyday, somewhat sordid setting, surrounded by a halo of dreams. The "Uni-Park" in *Pierrot, My Friend* is in many respects like a Parisian amusement park, and the descriptions of its attractions are scrupulously exact; Queneau, however, leads us not toward the amusement park at the Porte Maillot but toward a much more remote region.

All of Queneau's characters partake of a picturesque absurdity. Harum-scarums, city-dwelling Pierrots and Harlequins, layabouts hanging around the outskirts of the city, extravagant fairground figures—they are all out of step with real life, all misfits, loners. What is the meaning of this fragile world of outcasts, this social no-man's-land, this waste land? Queneau shows us how empty existence is when the cloak of "seriousness" is taken away. Pierrot is confronted by the same nothingness and the same absurd as Camus's Meursault or Sartre's Roquentin. And Queneau's humor is often the derisive laugh of one who knows bleakness too well. But the reflection of poetry on his characters is never altogether dissipated. And if death lurks behind Queneau's fairgrounds, behind the feast of words, it is easier to come face to face with death here, amid firecrackers and merry-go-rounds. Queneau shows sympathy and compassion toward a species of mankind which is ridiculous and doomed but which nevertheless retains the weapons of speech, dreams, and laughter.

Before Queneau, the novel had never been treated so freely, never been so "mixed up," so dislocated, to allow scope for all the rhythms and nuances of language; his work is a repository of linguistic structures that he constantly brings up to date. Language, forced out of its habitual mold, serves Queneau as magic without illusion, camouflaging the void without filling it. Language continues, however, to be a source of entertainment for a writer who, without being taken in by it, never tires of his inventiveness.

Jean Genet (born 1910), like Queneau, was an early contributor to *Les temps modernes* and became friendly with Sartre; indeed, Sartre wrote an important study of Genet, *Saint Genet, comédien et martyr* (1952, Saint Genet, Actor and Martyr). Like Queneau, Genet rejected society and its traditional forms of expression, and he, too, at the outset, accepted his marginal position and found his pleasure in the play of language. Genet's marginality, however, expressed itself in the direct confessions of *Journal du voleur* (1949, The Thief's Journal) and in fiction that was never very far from his actual experience: *Notre-Dame des Fleurs* (1948, Our Lady of the Flowers), *Miracle de la rose* (1944, Miracle of the Rose). And his language was not the spoken language but the language of poetic transfiguration.

In *The Thief's Journal* Genet explored the singularity of a particular kind of person—the homosexual thief: "Treachery, theft, and homosexuality are the basic subjects of this book. There is a relationship among them. . . ." Genet, speaking only of himself, was speaking for himself alone. He had no desire, as had Gide in *Corydon* (1911, 1920, Corydon), to proselytize or, like Queneau, to open the doors to a dream world that others could share: "Theft cannot give rise to a philosophy with politics and an ethics. Stealing is an activity I reserve for myself alone." These works of Genet's, which pushed individuality to the extreme, rejected any universalization, and their only general significance would have been as reportage, were it not for the power of the language. The light of poetry transformed the sinister and frightening underworld of pimps, murderers, and prostitutes. Bathed in this light, the worst filth took on a golden aura. Genet's style was something new in French writing: his supple prose was at the same time ornate and direct, ceremonial and simple, solemn and graceful, elevated and familiar.

In Genet's more recent work, particularly in his plays, he had modified and broadened his scope considerably. What has happened to him is what happens to most of those who start from negation: as they continue writing and living, they sooner or later convert negation into an affirmation; they create an ethical system, even if they do not wish to do so, by inverting their original values. That extreme limit, that purity of evil which Genet strove to attain like an ascetic, contained a challenge: "Saintliness is my goal. . . . I want to act so that everything I do may lead me to what is unknown to me." Why not, indeed, give the name of saintliness to the culmination of an effort infinitely more difficult than that associated with conventional morality since this effort isolates the person and does not tell him where it is leading?

The goal to be achieved was highly personal; though Genet may have felt linked to a given community it was one that—by definition—could not be universalized. In his recent plays, unlike his confessional narrative works, he has portrayed different kinds of minorities, for whom society bears the responsibility and who may appear as the spearhead of future society: the blacks, the third-world peoples. It is as if Genet had ended up by interpreting his own image as it had already been interpreted by his friends at *Les temps modernes*, as the symbol of social alienation. Going from himself (or his own kind) to others, he has thus moved toward universality. And he bridged the gap between the private world and the outer world by taking as the subject of his dramas people playing at being others or people playing at being themselves without succeeding—servants taking the role of their mistress in *Les bonnes* (1947, 1954, The Maids); blacks disguising themselves as whites in *Les nègres* (1958, The Blacks)—or people acting in private as they would like to behave in public, as in *Le balcon* (1956, The Balcony). The master has within him the slave, the slave the master, and rebellion leads to a communication and reveals an identity.

Can the theater help to transform the world he indicts,

or will his solution be to stop writing and, like Sartre—but for motives much closer to Artaud's—ally himself with the Black Panthers or with Arab guerrillas? After having accepted language and used it with a delight that was not without self-indulgence and affectation, Genet was tempted to reject it to the extent that it had no effect on his life. He once said that, despite the beauty of the words, the best western theater is nothing but "crap," since it fails to immerse us in the sacred, which is implicit in the ritual theater of Japan but which in western civilization is still most effectively evoked by the mass. Since it cannot be life, sacred life, literature is haunted by the specter of its own bankruptcy.

Michel Leiris has been associated with all the major intellectual currents since World War I: the poetic fervor of surrealism; the broad-scale inquiries of the school of sociological critics before World War II; the existentialist humanism of *Les temps modernes*; and the radical indictment of society that tends toward the renunciation of all literature for the sake of revolutionary action. Leiris's work has had great variety. Apart from the books he wrote as a professional ethnologist (*L'Afrique fantôme* [1934, Phantom Africa]), he also wrote important poetry.

But Leiris's most remarkable work, after his personal reminiscences in *L'âge d'homme* (1939, Manhood), is the autobiographical *La règle du jeu* (The Rules of the Game), which includes *Biffures* (1948, Erasures), *Fourbis* (1955, Gadgets), *Fibrilles* (1966, Fibrils). These books, which at first attracted few readers, have recently won a large audience. This self-portrait is illuminated and warmed by the sunshine of childhood; a self-analysis, it has plasticity, complexity, and precision. Leiris sometimes reminds one of Proust, but he expects from self-awareness a freeing and a transformation of the self; he wants to find the "rules of the game." These works, he said, "merely recount observations or experiences from which I hope to infer laws that will in the end reveal . . . the golden rule I ought to choose (or ought to have chosen) to direct my game."

But is this revelation not too late? Is there still time to discover in these forks in the road, erasures, and torn scraps—which require a great deal of patience to decipher—a direction that could be followed with less uncertainty in the future? If it is too late to make a new life for oneself, what can one do, except write? But writing has no meaning unless it leads somewhere, unless it is also living. The paradox of art is that, while it gives us an exaltation, the very exaltation indicates that art is only a symbol of something that transcends it.

In his preface to *Manhood* Leiris made some important remarks on "literature compared to the art of bullfighting." Literature must be a commitment, must risk life or death. The confession is in itself a kind of risk, and we sense what the author has had to overcome in order to draw an uncompromising self-portrait, laying bare his fundamental masochism and his own cowardice. But his life has been more than that; it has been governed throughout by a demand for poetry, by a desire for the exaltation of what "makes us cry out in wonder," the "going beyond the self," the "epilepsy" whose literary expression is justified only if it recaptures the authentic cry, the paradoxically ineffable moment of illumination.

In Leiris, language is the guiding thread, the culmination, but also the inadequacy. It is the guiding thread because through certain linguistic memories Leiris rediscovers his experience of life. In the child who said *"la fière"* (the proud) instead of *"la fièvre"* (the fever), the adult rediscovers the secrets of a world of poetry. But, in learning the real words, he realizes that there was someone else, the "interlocutor," for whom and with whom he had to speak. To go from *la fière* to la *fièvre* is to enter the objective world, and this progression reflects Leiris's social and political concerns, marked by his visits first to Cuba, then to China. How can the language of daily life be reconciled with the language of poetry? How can the dream be recaptured in deeds, in revolutionary action? The pathos and significance of Leiris's work lie in this dilemma, and we sense that the author would be ready to subscribe to the renunciation of literature were it not that he still believes in the possibility of a magical language capable of transforming the life of all. (And this belief reveals that vestiges of Leiris's old surrealist fervor still remain.)

Leiris's denunciation of language as an obstacle, as a convention to be destroyed, can be traced back to the surrealists' denunciation of rational language in favor of poetic language, which subsequently became a political denunciation of all alienated language. Maurice Blanchot reached somewhat the same conclusions about language, but by different paths and from a different starting point. Blanchot's work, difficult and enigmatic, is now becoming increasingly influential. He began publishing before the war, with critical studies later collected under the title *Faux-pas* (1943, False Step). These studies offered rigorous criticism of the realistic novel, which Blanchot accused of lagging behind poetry. "The essence of the novel," wrote Blanchot, "is to have its substance in its form," namely, in the movement of the words.

Blanchot's first novel, *Thomas l'obscur* (1941, Thomas the Obscure), was written somewhat in the style of Giraudoux, whom Blanchot the critic praised. But in *Aminadab* (1942, Aminadab) the influence of Giraudoux gave way to that of Kafka. Blanchot clearly did not regard language as an aesthetic exercise. And in his subsequent novels—*Le Très-Haut* (1948, The Almighty), *L'arrêt de mort*.(1948, Death Sentence), *Le dernier homme* (1957, The Last Man), *L'attente, l'oubli* (1962, Waiting, Forgetting)—which had an extraordinary tone of cold vehemence, an eloquence without eloquence, and a dispassionate shudder, Blanchot's style was neutral and impersonal. Rather than an individual or a writer, an anonymous witness speaks, conveying a truth that he sees as the only truth. It is a revelation that language has tried to express but which, in fact, it cannot express: the truth of the void, of absence, of nothingness, of death. This truth is perpetually waiting to be told but remains unsaid.

Everything in these works of Blanchot is situated in a strange, elusive, intermediate zone between life and death, in which life moves toward death but in which death cannot take place. This world between language and silence is like an almost mute downward slide, a movement that seems to lack motion and forever goes over the same ground. In his fiction Blanchot has presented the straining of language toward the "dangerous horizon where it seeks in vain to disappear"; he desires an inaccessible nonlanguage. He has commented on his quest in critical essays that have become more and more closely linked to his fiction, from *L'espace littéraire* (1955, Literary Space) to *L'entretien infini* (1970, Infinite Conversation).

The myth of Orpheus teaches us that we cannot look night in the face, that profundity is revealed only if it is concealed. But what good is this dissimulation, this constant fruitless searching for that which eludes us? The logic of the metaphysical experience (or mystical experience, but in a negative sense) has led Blanchot's work toward renunciation. Strangely enough, this tendency has been confirmed by a recent kind of revolutionary extremism, as if the unsaid were not only the forbidden area between life and death but also the area bourgeois civilization has forbidden to all of mankind, so that no one, for the moment, can speak for all men.

But the attempt to give a precise explanation of Blanchot's thought makes us run the risk of misrepresenting it. Blanchot's ideas can be grasped only in the way we appreciate music: by listening to it over and over again. The tenor of his thought always seems similar, but it eludes expression in words. Perhaps a clearer notion of Blanchot's work can be given by quoting some of the phrases that constitute the leitmotifs of one of his novels —say *Waiting, Forgetting*, which is perhaps his most difficult. "Help me to talk to you" is the initial plea; but in Blanchot's world speech no longer has the power of communication. "She was telling the truth, but not in what she said": truth lies behind or beside the meaning speech believes it is conveying. True speech is not philosophical interpretation, which "never stops talking," but the language of poetry, which is a language of contradiction—a voice, not the content of the words: "What she confided to you was her voice, and not what she said." And speech is not present but future, a groping toward a meaning that is then forgotten: "What was speaking in her was the approach, the approach to a word, the word of approach." Speech is thus a relationship with the unknown. But the unknown is not revealed; nor is it concealed. In a work of literature the unknown cannot reveal itself, lose its disguise, and cease to be what it is; but the literary work can be the "forefinger with a torn-off nail," through which the unknown is indicated as unknown. The mysterious insight that is brought near in such phrases disappears with them. We are in the realm of poetry, not of abstract thought.

Louis-René Des Forêts, whose work has been quantitatively small but highly significant, has followed paths similar to those of Blanchot. His early *Les mendiants* (1943, The Beggars) was, on the surface, a juxtaposition of monologues reminiscent of Faulkner. But Des Forêts made it clear that his central concern was much less the relativity of the different points of view (it is impossible to know what really happened from these contradictory accounts) than the power and credibility of speech itself. In *Le bavard* (1946, The Chatterbox) Des Forêts depicted a Dostoevskian fool who attempts, through constant invention, to hold our attention and to persaude us to accept what he says; but he does not succeed. The attempt of speech to enchant others or to achieve power condemns it to falsehood, and also condemns the writer (and all authority).

What is left then? Silence—unless a sudden reprieve is granted by song (and Des Forêts believes more in music than in literature) or by poetic inspiration, of which his *Les mégères de la mer* (1967, The Termagants of the Sea) was a recent example. The stories in his collection *La chambre des enfants* (1960, The Children's

Room), however, embodied most effectively Des Forêt's intractable dilemma. The adult who is listening at a door, behind which children are playing and talking of the secret rules governing their game, cannot hear or repeat what they are saying. Yet he knows that speech exists behind the door, transformed for the listener into a strangely disturbing echo, which sometimes lets him hope that he may hear what has been forbidden to him.

Marguerite Duras (born 1914) occupies a very special place in contemporary French fiction, insofar as she has been associated with various movements and currents, without really belonging to any of them. It has been said that her evolution offered a link between the existentialist novel and the *nouveau roman*. Duras began her career by publishing in Sartre's *Les temps modernes*, and a novel like *Les petits chevaux de Tarquinia* (1953, The Little Horses of Tarquinia) showed both an objectivity of writing style and a sharply accusing voice akin to the existentialists. Techniques of the *nouveau roman* can be seen in her later novels in dialogue form, such as *Le square* (1955, The Square), *Moderato contabile* (1958, Moderato Cantabile), and *Détruire, dit-elle* (1969, Destroy, She Said). In these novels, incoherent, obscure speech, fairly close to what Nathalie Sarraute (born 1900) has called "subconversation," suggests that the essential is encased in silence, that true speech, true communication, is impossible.

But Duras has also shown mastery in novels of a more traditional stamp, such as *Un barrage contre le Pacifique* (1950, A Dam against the Pacific); the theme of an extravagant, impossible love, always greater than the love actually experienced, is reminiscent of the surrealists's quest. Duras has also written some of the finest French

plays of the contemporary period. Her work is too complex to be associated with any one school, and if she
imitates particular techniques and lines of thought, she
does so in the spirit of a genuine eclectic, spontaneously
and unaffectedly. The world created by Duras has a dramatic force and an intensity of experience that give the
alternating voices, and even the silences separating them,
a tone that is immediately recognizable.

Except for Duras, most of the novelists I have just
discussed, especially Blanchot, altered fiction so much
that almost nothing of the traditional novel remained.
Their works can often be better described as stylistic,
autobiographical exercises, disembodied narratives in
which the "character" is merely an anonymous voice and
the action is merely the path described by the words.
These writers did not attempt to define new laws for the
novel but rather to find any means of expressing something essential, the quest for which led to an awareness
of the inexpressible. This bursting of the bounds of the
novel, and even of literature itself, perhaps found its most
decisive expression in the work of Georges Bataille.

The almost boundless curiosity and vast erudition of
Georges Bataille, who was the director of the Collège de
Sociologie and of the review *Documents* before he founded
the review *Critique*, enabled him to explore many different areas of thought. He wrote essays on subjects ranging
from sociology, political science, and economics in *La
part maudite* (1949, The Cursed Part), to aesthetics in
Manet (1955, Manet) and *Lascaux, ou la naissance de
l'art* (1955, Lascaux, or the Birth of Art), to psychoanalysis, and even to numismatics. We can see in the
relationships he suggested among such distinct fields the

first signs of the structuralist approach; indeed, the structuralists of today still acknowledge their debt to Bataille. Whatever he had to say was subordinated to the same quest. This intensity of the quest was amplified in his philosophical investigations in *L'expérience intérieure* (1943, Inner Experience) and *Le coupable* (1944, The Guilty One), and in his fiction: *L'anus solaire* (1931, The Solar Anus); *Madame Edwarda* (1937, Mrs. Edwarda), which was first published under a pseudonym; *L'abbé C* (1950, Abbé C); and *Le bleu du ciel* (The Blue of the Sky), published in 1957 but written much earlier.

In Bataille's fiction the narrative sometimes takes the form of a myth, sometimes of an apparently realistic account. Sometimes it explodes into a series of isolated fragments of existentialist philosophy, as in *Histoire de rats* (1947, Story of Rats). Bataille used a violent, taut, abrupt approach to express the tension of a life always seeking the extreme states in which truth, man's movement toward the absolute, could burst forth in both pleasure and pain, in eroticism and death.

Bataille turned his back completely on the world of ordinary, sometimes insignificant events, the empty moments of life that Breton had condemned in those novels that used them as their raw material. Bataille was interested only in moments of ecstasy, of excess. "Only the choking, intolerable experience allows the author to reach the distant vision expected by a reader weary of the narrow limits imposed by conventions. How can we waste time on books that the author has clearly not been compelled to write?" Thus wrote Bataille in the preface to *The Blue of the Sky*, which is, however, the novel in which he most conforms to traditional narrative form.

Eroticism, a profane mystique, and a longing after the sacred elements of primitive civilizations were all attempts of Bataille's to break into a domain in which the rational, partial sense is lost, in which life and language come up against the impossibility of finding an order and continuing. The sudden appearance of a key experience breaks the continuity of the narrative. But the unity of this experience enables us to reconstitute the dispersed aphorisms and lengthy meditations in which Bataille, ignoring continuity and structure, relentlessly pursued his search for expression.

Bataille wrote in fragments as Nietzsche wrote in aphorisms, but the fragments are linked by a similarity of emotion rather than by structure or by an intellectual dialectic. In Bataille's work, the fragmentary mode of writing used by Pascal and Nietzsche came into its own. Pascal's notes were intended as a basis for a coherent apologia, and Nietzsche's for a systematic treatise. For them, the fragment was merely a temporary expedient; for Bataille, it was a deliberately chosen form, the only one suitable to his thought. Bataille did not wish either to demonstrate or to construct; he was not concerned with communicating knowledge or a system. He did not speculate on an experience in order to convert it into thought; he *was* his experience, and he had to express it in its entirety at the first attempt. Moreover, his experience was such that it could not take an intellectual form, because it was an awareness of that primordial unity which thought must inevitably destroy, because thought implies division. Bataille's inner experience was the experience of not knowing.

Bataille was not, like Nietzsche, a contradictory thinker

hesitating between positions but finding contradiction an embarrassment, a provisional stage of thought. Bataille was a thinker of contradiction, or rather of unity. His thoughts did not conflict with one another; they overlapped. He was not torn by contradiction, but by division. He did not seek a vision of the world or an ethical principle that would enable him to go beyond contradiction by establishing a hierarchy of values. Instead he strove to find an experience to unify all contradictions; he sought the source. He was closer to the mystics than to the Hegelians because he rejected everything that was relative or limited, everything that resembled an object or a purpose. He was seeking the *sovereign experience*, the experience that cannot be subordinated to anything.

Bataille contrasted this experience with political, ethical, and aesthetic activities, calling his experience, in turn, inner experience, ecstacy, rapture, immediacy and contact with the nakedness of being; it was a kind of explosion of the individual in an all-embracing void. The states and means he favored in his meditation—laughter, eroticism, intoxication, poetry, the primitive feast, and sacrifice—were all forms of communication by which man transcends his divided self. "I imagine that the world does not resemble any separate and self-enclosed being, but whatever it is that passes from one to another when we laugh, when we love." The reader can understand the significance of Bataille's obsession with death: it is the final rapture, the transition into absolute immanence.

Sartre called Bataille a latter-day mystic. But Bataille's inner experience was an experience without God; God appeared to him as an object, a specific end, a principle of relativity, an obstacle to absolute freedom. Bataille explained that his method was also diametrically opposed to yoga, since yoga is a complex of methods and practices binding one to the very sphere of activity from which it claims to free the individual. Yet, for all his concern for achieving unity, what makes Bataille so interesting today is not so much his quest as the very individual system of obsessions related to it. The depth and significance Bataille gave to the themes of intoxication, of laughter, and of nostalgia for the primitive rites—sacrifices, feasting, and barter—clearly separated his work from any banal form of mysticism.

One may legitimately wonder how Bataille was able to come down from the "sovereign experience" to the mundane world of revolutionary political thought? For Bataille has this interest as well, and he devoted a great many essays to the structures of fascism, communism, and capitalism; and he always made specific political choices. Although it is hard to reconcile these two sides of Bataille, it must be pointed out that in none of his work did Bataille look for shortcuts; he opened up the whole range of contemporary thought. He heralded contemporary thought by rejecting all counterfeits, all the meanings that humanism was content to accept. No one has better expressed the realization that everything that has been said is silent on what there is to say; no one has better cleared the ground.

Bataille was nonetheless separated from the writers who have tended toward a despairing slide into silence; the brilliance of the imagery could be heard in his shattered voice. He was the romantic precursor of a literature that was to become a cold and abstruse machine. He may have been the poet of the "hatred of poetry." But Bataille, who indeed wrote *La haine de la poésie* (1947, Hatred of Poetry), was himself a poet.

Eroticism, profane mysticism, the search for the absolute—all these elements permit one to draw parallels between Bataille and Pierre Klossowski (born 1905), who, like Bataille, also wrote on Nietzsche and Sartre. But Klossowski is a Catholic, although in heretical guise; moreover, his complex works of fiction are written in slow legato lines, in contrast to Bataille's staccato rhythms. In Klossowski's works, nothing is immediately obvious; there is always a palimpsest to be deciphered, an operation that presupposes extensive theoretical and scholastic knowledge. The situations he describes create uneasiness, distress, and anguish, but one is aware that they are the means to a spiritual experience.

In Klossowski's work everything appears to converge on the relationships between the soul and the body. All the perversities and erotic aberrations depicted in *Roberte ce soir* (1950, Roberte This Evening), *La révocation de l'Édit de Nantes* (1959, The Revocation of the Edict of Nantes), and *Le Baphomet* (1965, Baphomet) are undoubtedly merely a way of destroying or annihilating the body. If the soul is to be saved, then the body must no longer be bound by prohibitions of any kind. And yet Klossowski seems to have become more and more aware that even the door to the mind is barred by countless prohibitions. Man is stifled, buried beneath his fellow men, beneath the density of tradition and language; and the movement toward freedom or toward the absolute has to be an endless striving, first to decipher, then to destroy. Yet everything that can be destroyed is only a symbol. Therefore, when this sadistic destruction is completed, there is hope of finding the indestructable.

Jean Paulhan should be included with the foregoing writers, not so much because of his fiction, most of which was written long before World War II (*Le guerrier appliqué* [1915, The Industrious Warrior], *Aytré qui perd l'habitude* [1921, Aytré Loses the Habit], *La guérison sévère* [1925, The Rigorous Cure]), but because of the influence he exerted on all literature as director of the *Nouvelle revue française* after the death of Jacques Rivière (1886–1925).

At first sight, there is no common link between Paulhan's essays and the works I have just discussed. The style, tone, content, and ideological implications of Paulhan's work seem diametrically opposed to that of writers whom he discovered and defended. His style had a classical elegance; indeed, Paulhan dedicated *Les fleurs de Tarbes* (1941, The Flowers of Tarbes) to André Gide. His tone was ironically allusive. His goal seemed to be a rehabilitation of rhetoric. And his political views tended toward conservative nationalism. But the contradiction between the apparent meaning of Paulhan's own work and his enthusiasm for writers so different from himself should serve as a clue to the secrets of his own work.

Paulhan's thought is "dated" in that it was concerned with the state of current literature, which was (and still is) a state of crisis. Everything, Paulhan felt, pointed to a crisis: the estrangement of the public from literature; the contradictions of the critics; the divergence of doctrines; the disintegration of the relationship between the writer and his reader, with the result that the reader found artificial what the writer believed sincere, that the listener experienced as metaphor what to the speaker seemed the object itself, or as a cliché what the author felt to be a spontaneous discovery and a new image. The crisis was such that the writer, after having thought himself a god, is now tempted by silence and even suicide, so inadequate and bungling does he find language and the techniques of his art.

Paulhan, in describing all the manifestations of this crisis, referred to it as the "Terror." The "terrorist" writer considers himself as suspect, or rather he considers as suspect all the means employed by a language in which he no longer has any confidence. The terrorist no longer trusts words; he refrains from using a rhetoric devalued by usage and therefore unable to express the special message within him. He refuses to seek assistance in the established rules of the genres, because genre seems as outworn as rhetoric. He rejects beauty, because he is seeking something other than beauty. Thus, the Terror is aimed at nothing less than the destruction of literature.

Paulhan refrained from proposing any solution, and he had no illusions about the harm wrought by rhetoric; he knew full well that rhetoric was responsible for the existence of the Terror. Yet he destroyed some of the assumptions of the Terror. He demonstrated very clearly how what is regarded as a cliché is not a cliché for the writer, but sincere expression. He showed persuasively that concepts of genre did have an enduring value and that the flowers of rhetoric, like the flowers of Tarbes, have their attraction. More generally, he made it clear that there can be no literature without an act of faith in language. Paulhan felt that it was a mistake to believe that in order to be original, sincere, and complete, literary expression must reject the framework and support of language; if we struggle against language, the struggle will absorb all our strength. Nothing will remain but language, and we shall no longer succeed in saying anything about ourselves. To accept language is the only way to express the truth one wishes to convey. If language is our ally, we shall not fall into the trap of verbalism; if it is our adversary, our only choice is verbalism or silence. If thought revolves around language, thought is liberated by language. "If I rebel, I shall be enslaved; if I am meek, I shall be master."

The acceptance of language liberates the mind, because mind and language are both made of the same matter. This is what Paulhan hinted at in *Clef de la poésie* (1944, Key to Poetry), in which he offered a continuation of *The Flowers of Tarbes*. Paulhan always started from the same contradiction. Some approach poetry as rhetoricians, others as terrorists. For some, poetry is inspiration, an experience that transcends language; for others, it is tied to language. For some, poetry is a sound, for others a sign; for some, it is matter, for others mind. In other words, poetry can be viewed in two ways, and this ambivalence is found in the linguist who sometimes treats thought as language, sometimes treats language as thought. How can this contradiction be explained except by saying that these two viewpoints are equally false and equally well-founded. Not that language is on the one hand mind and on the other matter, or that poetry is on the one hand sound and on the other meaning. To arrive at the truth, the two viewpoints must not be superimposed; they must cancel each other out. In life, the mysterious but precise and inextricable relationship between language and thought leads us to conclude that they cannot be distinguished, that they are in some way identical. In poetry, form and substance are not superimposed, but reversible and interchangeable.

"In the end, I have said nothing": this is the last sentence of *The Flowers of Tarbes*. It warns us against any restrictive interpretation of an open-minded work, in which Paulhan was content to show us language both as literature and as illusion and ambiguity. Standing alone because of his subtle academism and formal charm, Paulhan offered a necessary prelude and parallel to those "barbarian" and "nonformal" works that, by attacking language, have burst the bounds of literature, first and foremost in the novel.

Although in recent years writers have questioned every assumption of the novel, an important group of them has defined and exemplified new rules for it instead of abandoning it. It is almost as if a reconstruction has followed the revolutionary violence. But before discussing the reconstruction—the *nouveau roman*—I would like to consider the individualistic, although related, contribution of Samuel Beckett. Born in Dublin, like James Joyce, who had a very great influence on him, Beckett began writing in English before he wrote in French; he remains a bilingual writer in that he himself translates most of his French works into English and in that he still occasionally writes a major work in English (such as *Happy Days* [1961], which he translated into French as *Oh les beaux jours* [1963]). Beckett shares existentialism's pessimistic vision and the somewhat despairing use of language evidenced in the writers previously discussed.

Beckett's works occupy a zone between the absurd and silence. Novels such as *Molloy* (1950, Molloy), *Malone meurt* (1951, Malone Dies), *L'innommable* (1953, The Unnamable), and *Comment c'est* (1960, How It Is) were as far removed from the traditional novel as such plays as *En attendant Godot* (1953, Waiting for Godot), *Fin de partie* (1957, Endgame), and *Happy Days* were from any theatrical tradition. But Beckett was not interested in the theoretical redefinition of the novel that younger writers were pursuing. His singularity and his greatness rest in his ability to sustain genuine creation in an almost total void, giving spontaneity and richness to what he retained of the basic elements of the novel and the drama.

It is true that nothing happens in Beckett's novels; we do not know where they take place, and an anonymous voice talks endlessly of what it is unable to name. A consciousness condemned to talk in vain, because it cannot find the final word that would enable it to return to silence, harps endlessly on the same theme. This final "word" is not a truth that would put an end to speech by giving it an object; it is the disappearance of all objects—nothingness. This endless murmuring belongs to a being that is forced to talk to itself as long as it lives a life that looks to death as the only release and suffers at being separated from it. This voice is the murmuring of existence itself, at its most secret and also at its most universal. Nothing remains in the world except this perpetual voice, incapable of seeing, of identifying, or of explaining. There is no here, no now, no yesterday (the near-impossibility of reconstituting a memory is one of the constant themes of Beckett's novels), no I, no you, no he. Beckett captures moments when everything seems about to come to an end, in a faded twilight, in the half-light of the blind.

In Beckett's plays, too, nothing happens. The characters wait for someone, like Godot, who does not come; or the infirm look at one another, resigned to an intolerable situation that has no end. "The end is in the beginning, and yet we go on," says one character in *Endgame*. In *Happy Days* a woman whose body is gradually sinking into the ground until only her head remains recalls insignificant memories and strings together phrases so banal that they lose all sense.

In Beckett's works, unlike those of some of the younger writers, the idea is still given a concrete form. Molloy and Malone show themselves, through their monologues, to be monstrous invalids in whom life is revealed in its worst physiological tyranny; they are witnesses of the impotent horror of being bodies. In Beckett's plays the voice becomes divided, and its several forms engage in dialogue, confront situations. A sadomasochistic relationship, the relationship of master and slave, links characters in *Waiting for Godot* and those in *Endgame*. Although nothing happens, there is a mounting tension and sometimes even a kind of hope: if Godot were to arrive, if death were to retreat, if happy days were to return, everything would be transformed. None of this happens, but the tension sustains the action on stage; Beckett succeeds in keeping his audience in suspense to the very end.

In recent French literature Beckett is the only one who has shown us that while the novel or play can divest itself of all its outward appearances and conventions, to remain a true creation it must preserve a movement, a tension, that compels the reader or audience to go on reading or listening, page after page, scene after scene. This tension derives from a mystery of creation no intellectual redefinitions of literature can ever completely dispel.

4

FROM THE NOUVEAU ROMAN TO TEXTUAL WRITING

The most important recent development in fiction has been what is called the *nouveau roman*. But is there a new novel? Its existence is often disputed by those who stress the diversity, and even the incompatibility, of the writers grouped under this label: those who have redefined the novel as an "observation," a description, seem far removed from those who explore the inner world of the "unspoken." Yet, despite the divergences and individual modes of its practitioners, there are undoubtedly common features.

During the mid-1950s critics and readers became aware that the novel was taking a new direction, which they associated with the publishing house of Les Éditions de Minuit (previously, almost all important French novels were published by Gallimard). The reactions to these Éditions de Minuit novels were extreme: people either rejected them because of their novelty and difficulty, or accepted them out of perspicacity or snobbishness. The novels that elicited these reactions were: in 1953, *Les gommes* (The Erasers) by Alain Robbe-Grillet (born 1922) and *Martereau* (Martereau) by Nathalie Sarraute; in 1954, *Passage de Milan* (Milan Passage) by Michel Butor (born 1926); in 1957, *La jalousie* (Jealousy) by Robbe-Grillet, *La modification* (The Change) by Michel Butor, which was awarded the Prix Renaudot, and *Le vent* (The Wind) by Claude Simon (born 1913). There almost simultaneously appeared essays that resembled manifestos: *Le roman comme recherche* (1955, The Novel as Research) by Butor; *Conversation et sous-conversation* (1956, Conversation and Subconversation) by Sarraute; *Une voie pour le roman futur* (1956, A Way for the Novel of the Future) and *Nature, humanisme et tragédie* (1958, Nature, Humanism, and Tragedy) by Robbe-Grillet.

This movement, which extends from precursors like Beckett to disciples just now beginning to write, has acquired widespread interest and general acceptance. For example, Jacqueline Piatier, a writer for the newspaper *Le monde*, in discussing the publication of Claude Simon's ninth novel, *La bataille de Pharsale* (1969, The Battle of Pharsalus), clearly stated that the *nouveau roman* was something other than a fringe phenomenon:

> The crown [the Nobel Prize] awarded to Beckett and the growing prestige of Claude Simon point in any event to the worldwide recognition now accorded to the *nouveau roman*. It has surely been sufficiently attacked in France under the banners of defunct classicism and renascent surrealism. But if we look back on the literature of the last ten years, we are bound to acknowledge that the Édi-

tions de Minuit stable has given us the most representative, the most consistent, and the most
innovative writers of our age—and, it must be
added, the most fertile. In none of them does there
seem to be any danger of a drying up of inspiration.

What do these new novelists have in common? First,
they are literary *artists* (even if they dislike the term),
whereas Sartre and Camus wrote primarily to advance an
ethical or political position, to expound a truth. ("I write
to find out why I write," Robbe-Grillet has said.) For
the new novelists, the links between literary endeavor and
social problems are indirect, sometimes almost nonexist-
ent. In this, the new novelists have somewhat resembled
the art-for-art's-sake writers of the turn of the century.
And this characteristic of the *nouveau roman* can be explained fairly well by historical circumstances: immediately after the Liberation, politics in France was a vital
force that seemed on the verge of dominating literature;
then (with the Algerian war, the prompt return to the
politics of the past, the disappointments over socialist
governments in other countries) politics lost its grip on
writers' imaginations and was replaced by more purely
literary concerns.

Another characteristic of the Éditions de Minuit writers was that they were novelists in the strict sense of the
word (this is what separates them from writers such as
Blanchot, who in so many other respects, especially the
preoccupation with language, paved the way for them).
As novelists, this new group of writers, which included
Robbe-Grillet, Sarraute, and the others, resumed the attempt, begun and abandoned by Sartre, to give a new
set of laws to the novel, which they regarded as the major

genre—if not the only genre! Their realization that the possibilities of the traditional novel had been exhausted did not lead them to burst open its bounds and overlap all genres. Instead, they pursued a redefinition, not by drafting a joint manifesto but by producing a sufficiently similar body of fictional and theoretical work. They regarded their essayist activities as solely in the service of their novels. For them, the novel and essay were not equivalent forms of expression, subordinated to a truth that transcended both genres.

The point of departure for this new set of laws was, nonetheless, the barrenness of the traditional novel, whose presumptions had never been questioned so clearly. When, in *L'ère du soupçon* (1956, The Age of Suspicion), Nathalie Sarraute insisted that there was no longer any possibility of keeping the reader in suspense through some exciting plot, of establishing lifelike characters, of describing a natural or social setting, or even of giving new analyses of human emotions (since the tradition of Benjamin Constant was no less exhausted than that of Balzac), she was acting as a spokesman for them all, even though her reasons may not have been identical with theirs. The narrative would no longer follow the continuity of a story or of time; it would no longer depict recognizable characters with whom we are tempted to identify ourselves; it would no longer describe in detail a setting or a scene essential for comprehension of the action. Time, reality, and people would henceforth be conveyed in discontinuous, scrambled flashes. In short, for the first time, a systematic and common effort was made to remove from the novel the bones (story, characters, and also meaning) to which the flesh used to adhere, so that nothing but the flesh remained.

As in abstract painting, in the *nouveau roman* the forms of organization disappeared and matter, matter itself, took their place (except that in the novel the forms of organization were not the object or the model, but the plot, the character, and so forth). And even though this matter is preeminently concrete, the *nouveau roman*, like some painting, appears to be abstract because we feel that an effort is being made to exclude elements regarded as stale or impure, in favor of elements regarded as untouched or pure; previously the novel had been a spontaneous mixture of forms of organization and matter (of a manifest and a latent content). Thus, the *nouveau roman* is abstract because it removes something—and does so intentionally; because it reduces the world to a single idea of the world. (This intense need to experiment, to push a possibility to its extreme, is a tendency not uncommon in the history of French literature, the prime examples being classicism and naturalism.)

Thus, the establishment of a new set of laws for the novel was not, as it was for Sartre, based on the reduction of the visual field; it was rather the radicalization of all elements, the logical end of an evolution to which James Joyce had contributed so much. The dismissal of the traditional novel was unequivocal. But what did this dismissal mean? It was not enough for these writers to say that the forms were outworn because they had been used too much; for them, the forms were not appropriate for new world conditions or for what always used to be left unsaid. What was eliminated was an approach that no longer captured reality, an approach dictated by a particular set of values and by a particular mode of writing; to follow the old approach was to accept that what one writes has already been written. Although Sartre was content to elaborate a metaphysical system in his novels ("All techniques refer back to a metaphysical system," he said), and he accepted the existence of thought and means of expression as prior to composition, the new novelists have been unanimous in advocating and practicing a mode of writing that rejects any ready-made meanings or rhetorical devices, since they feel they would otherwise be condemned merely to repeat what has already been written.

The discontinuity, the disintegration of the action and of time, and the fragmentation of consciousness in the novel thus ensured a more nearly complete and a more precise picture than the macroscopic treatment. But this completeness meant, at the same time, a suspension of meaning. A traditional treatment prejudges, gives an *a priori* meaning; it obscures or dilutes the vision of the thing itself by attaching a meaning to it. It is like talking about something rather than showing it; we read the caption instead of seeing the picture. We must, said Robbe-Grillet, let the "world speak for itself." The traditional novel had merely "spoken about the world." The object must emerge and manifest itself directly, without any intervention, without the analytical, explanatory voice of the narrator. The words must act as objects; they are objects. And the order of the words must follow simply the sequence of their appearance, not a sequence dominated from beginning to end by a conscious mind. (But insofar as there is succession and continuity, is a conscious mind not postulated?) An ordered vision of the world, or rather a preordered vision—whether stemming from theology, humanism, or bourgeois conformism— was thus followed by a disordered vision. Is it disordered because disorder is inherent in the universe, or because it does not really contain any meaning, or because it is waiting for a new order to be established? It would seem that the meaning that has been withdrawn is replaced only by the meaning of the writing itself. The narrative patently plays with its own structures, which are elements of language much more than elements of reality, as if the form related only to itself, to the act of creation. Furthermore, if the fragmented yet omnipresent consciousness in these novels is no longer that of a character, it must be that of narrator. This narrator, to be sure, is no longer present to "speak of the world" and comment on his view of the world; he is there to write, and sometimes even to comment on the act of writing. In other words, the narrator is no longer the interpreter of what has already been written; he is instead the agent of a work in progress.

To resolve any ambiguity about the nature of this kind of fiction, some of these writers have written novels that tell the very story of their own narration, with the result that the book being read simultaneously seems in the process of being written. Is the *nouveau roman* thus a new formalism, a contemporary manifestation of art for art's sake? Perhaps. But one could also claim that meaning is suspended rather than suppressed, that the writing aims at filling the void created by the absence of meaning. It does so not by offering itself as the final meaning but by setting in motion a movement aimed toward identifying, even if obliquely, the meanings and values of an alienated society and illustrating a new relationship between the individual and the world. Is this aesthetic solipsism, or realism starting from a blank state? The *nouveau roman* seems to oscillate between these two possibilties, these two temptations.

Having noted these points in common, I can further

define the new novelists only by pointing to their differences. The contrasts between Nathalie Sarraute and Alain Robbe-Grillet are particularly striking. For Sarraute, psychological reality, the inner world, has remained the goal. Her method of investigating this reality is not, however, the kind of analysis that establishes character once and for all, transforms the living into something dead, and treats states of mind divorced from actions. Nor has her means been the interior monologue. Since for Sarraute psychological reality is inseparable from behavior, she has used dialogue. But her dialogue is not that of ordinary conversation. It is the dialogue of the unsaid, of what she terms the "subconversation." Through these subconversations she tries to capture those inner movements through which we react to others and to ourselves (she calls these inner movements "tropisms"). By means of these techniques Sarraute wants to give the reader the "illusion of reenacting events himself with greater awareness, with more order, clarity, and force than he can in real life, yet without the events losing the qualities of indetermination, opacity, and mystery that they always have for the one who is actually experiencing them."

Robbe-Grillet's reply to Sarraute was that her approach was still anthropomorphic, that it still postulated its own reality, which makes us lose sight of the only reality with which we should be concerned—the reality of appearance itself, the reality of the object: "The operation that she [Sarraute] attempts to impose on the world threatens to dissolve and annihilate it completely. In neglecting the surface of things for an ever more distant, ever more inaccessible depth, is one not forced to reach only shadows, reflections, patches of mist?"

For Robbe-Grillet, the novel had to cease being *emo-*

tional, metaphorical, or *spell-binding,* had to become *visual* and *descriptive.* Whether realistic or romantic, the traditional novel endeavored to discover reality beneath appearances; and that reality was always presented as meaningful. Robbe-Grillet felt that recent novels of the absurd were making a similar mistake in having non-meaning as their specific content. We have discovered, he said, that the "world is neither significant nor absurd; it simply *is.*" And Robbe-Grillet set out to describe this state of being, this *"is."*

The differences between Robbe-Grillet and Sarraute can be further seen in their choice of mentors. The novelists who have served as points of reference for Robbe-Grillet are Flaubert and Kafka, Joyce and Raymond Roussel (1877–1933). Sarraute's models have been Dostoevski, Virginia Woolf, and Ivy Compton-Burnett.

Sarraute's first work was published as early as 1938; it was a little book entitled *Tropismes* (Tropisms), which went almost completely unnoticed but which nevertheless contained a number of elements she was later to draw on. *Tropisms* consists of very short texts in which a consciousness that is never named, an almost impersonal point of reference, opens itself or draws back in reaction to a stimulus from without, sometimes taking on a coloration that allows it to be glimpsed. In 1947 she published *Portrait d'un inconnu* (Portrait of a Man Unknown), which Sartre described in his foreword as an anti-novel, but which was much more of a novel than *Tropisms,* because there is an organization of its discontinuities. And in *Martereau, Le planétarium* (1959, The Planetarium), and *Les fruits d'or* (1963, The Golden Fruits) something resembling a story is unfolded, bringing into conflict characters of a sort: a foolish young man who wants to be an artist, a maniacal aunt, a divided family, a famous woman writer seen both in her moments of glory and in her moments of absurdity, and so on. But the stories and the characters are not in themselves important; they are used to bring to light what has hitherto not been revealed, what has remained *unspoken* or has been obscured by the cruder interests of other writers, and to create a more subtle and a more profound order.

Sarraute's reader, therefore, cannot follow a continuous narrative or pattern of behavior; he must at every point be sensitive to minute movements, to reactions that elude him, to words that evaporate or become submerged. Like the antennae of an insect, the nervous, ductile language —with few images but many verbs—detects the slightest modifications, the slightest undulations in the terrain. That Sarraute had to equip herself with this more sensitive instrument did not necessarily mean that a new, more subtle reality had come into being, but rather that the old reality had never been fully explored, that the unsaid had always remained hidden behind the glibness of speech.

Sarraute transformed writing not, as I said, so much in response to a new historical situation as in an attempt to deal with a problem found in any society: the problem of inauthenticity. Her characters are always caught up in sham behavior: snobbishness, conventional judgments, social mimesis, false perception of character. The sham robs their words of truth, while someone—a part of them, or another consciousness?—rejects these false words and continually keeps an ear open for other, whispered words. And individuality is one of these shams: the movement of words in Sarraute's novels suggests the dance of an anonymous consciousness. Is there a meaning, a truth? There may be, but only in some inaccessible realm, not as a meaning that we can possess or define—only as a meaning toward which we can grope, the meaning of a movement of the consciousness, the act of writing itself.

While Sarraute's early books often had a manifest subject—usually intellectuality and literary consciousness—that could be separated from the latent content, in her recent *Entre la vie et la mort* (1968, Between Life and Death), which recounts the total activity of the creation of a book, she fused the surface themes completely with the underlying themes. The anecdote, which was formerly a mediation between writer and reader, disappeared, as did almost all the remnants of tradition found in her earlier novels. The foreword to *Between Life and Death* gives us this warning:

> The reader who follows his normal habit of looking everywhere for characters, who wastes his time trying to pigeonhole the sensations or tropisms that make up the substance of this book, will realize that his efforts to allocate them properly have led him to construct a hero made up of disparate parts, which do not really hang together.

Yet Sarraute did not return to the absolute discontinuity of her early *Tropisms*. Although her novels are becoming increasingly pared down and are moving nearer and nearer to the extreme of experimentation, they nevertheless remain this side of the limit and, despite abstractness, retain a potential dramatic movement that is constantly reborn out of their fragmentation.

Alain Robbe-Grillet's collection *Instantanés* (Snapshots), which was published in 1962 but which contained much earlier writings, had a role in his work similar to that of *Tropisms* in the work of Nathalie Sarraute. It contained all the elements that he has since used, in more complex and expanded form, in the construction of his novels. In Robbe-Grillet's work these elements are not the movement of a consciousness or of inchoate speech but rather series of still lifes, rigorously framed, coldly and pitilessly described, which exclude any nonvisual notation, any epithet acting as a vehicle for a human reaction or assessment. ("The coffee pot is on the table.") And undoubtedly this pure presence of objects, this world of pure appearances—with the descriptive element reigning supreme, no longer subordinated to the narrative— is the most striking thing about Robbe-Grillet's novels and constitutes their trademark.

Yet, while it is understandable that by means of the cinema, to which Robbe-Gillet has devoted himself more and more, he wanted to go beyond the written presence of the image (and even to substitute an absence for a presence), it is less easy to see what his novels have added to the texts in *Snapshots*, if his project is solely descriptive. They are anti-novels in a sense, because the story undermines a conventional form: the detective story in *The Erasers* and *Le voyeur* (1955, The Voyeur), the commonplace story of adultery in *La jalousie* (1957, Jealousy), and the adventure story in *Dans le labyrinthe* (1959, In the Labyrinth). Yet these works are novels, because the very form that is denounced and contested acts as a guiding thread, as a frame of reference, as a magnetic pole. The object described, scoured of all meaning, wiped of all human traces, does not obstruct or satisfy our imagination; instead, it has an unbearable unreality, which makes us need and expect the meaning that it has been deprived of. It seems to be the opening word of a story which is hidden from us but whose presence we continually suspect.

Admittedly, the meaning to which the object refers in turn refers back to the object, and this detour may be only the proof *ad absurdum* of the exclusive reality of the object as object. But for Robbe-Grillet's proof to be decisive, it is essential that we finally succeed in seeing the object without its halo, without its anthropomorphic or narrative dramatic potential. We do not, however, read *Jealousy* in the way we read the truly discontinuous texts of *Snapshots*. Robbe-Grillet did not succeed in exorcising the suggestion of narrative, because there are undertones of action in the description. Nor did he succeed in making this description itself a truly objective vision, for even if the description does not arise out of a narrative, it is nonetheless prompted by personal obsessions.

Personal obsessions are becoming more and more evident in Robbe-Grillet's work, and ultimately the play of these obsessions has replaced the earlier pretext of a narrative through parody of traditional forms. In *La maison de rendez-vous* (1965, The House of Assignation), and even more so in *Projet pour une révolution à New York* (1970, Project for a Revolution in New York), the narrative framework that had still supported *Jealousy* and *The Voyeur* disappeared altogether. In *Project for a Revolution in New York* the story is completely destroyed in that the same beginnings of a plot constantly reappear in different contexts. Time no longer has any before or after; it is the motionless time of a memory containing only juxtaposed images, countless simultaneous sensations of an impersonal consciousness. Yet there is a progression in the text, which is punctuated by the phrase "And now . . . ," suggesting a movement in time. But the image returned to is often the same, or a slight variation of the same image; reality in this novel is not the movement of time but the rotation or "revolution" of a combination of images.

These images, which are not necessitated by the unfolding of an action, must clearly be prompted by Robbe-Grillet's personal obsessions that are the real "generating themes" of a novel without subject or chronology. They are images taken from the "mythological material" of day-to-day life (eroticism, violence, and all the symbols of social alienation). Indeed, *Project for a Revolution in New York* is a montage of scenes and posters of the streets of New York, an example of "pop art." These elements, the author tells us, are not to be either rejected or exalted; they are insignificant in themselves and take on meaning only through the montage, through the structural interplay we can imagine. The reader's only liberty lies in the margin afforded by this interplay.

Robbe-Grillet thus broke with all realism, because the work of fiction finds its generating principle only in itself. But the break is ambiguous, because the fiction is made up solely of insignificant elements. And it is not even clear whether all these elements are on the same plane. Rearranging them may well be the only thing left to do, in view of their significance. It may also be a way for the reader to accentuate those elements he can identify with; eroticism, for example, is a real experience before it is an imaginative interplay of formal structures. Whatever one's reaction is to the content of *Project for a Revolution in New York*, one must admit that its style is marked by an elliptical sharpness, a restraint, and a control that relate Robbe-Grillet's writing itself to a tradition that is very French.

The almost simultaneous appearance of the first works of Robbe-Grillet and those of Michel Butor created the impression of a new *school*, rather than of innovative individuals. But it is becoming increasingly difficult to link these two writers together. Moreover, Butor has taken a theoretical stand very different from Robbe-Grillet's. Rather than trying to find a new definition of limited scope for the novel, Butor has pursued a wide-ranging, ambitious quest extending to the whole of literature. (The French word *"recherche,"* which Butor used to describe his literary program, means "research" in the sense of searching anew, of quest.)

Butor's quest is based less on a feeling that the old forms of expression are worn out than on a feeling that these forms are too narrow and too restricted to express a world that had become extraordinarily enlarged. The writer is thus forced to forge new means of expression. "The quest for new forms of the novel with greater power of integration thus plays the triple role of denunciation, exploration, and adaptation, in relation to our awareness of reality," he wrote in *The Novel as Research*. Butor's denunciation was not only literary; the old forms, repeated out of laziness, which were blind or untruthful, went hand in hand with a conservative social order. But Butor's main stress was on adaptation; reality, which for Robbe-Grillet was—in an ambiguous way—to be annulled and then used, and for Nathalie Sarraute was to be pursued in the form of authenticity, was for Butor the subject of an optimistic, wonder-struck exploration. He is like Claudel, but with a dry, brittle lyricism. And it is worth noting the importance for both Claudel and

Butor of the myth of a "new world," without which the universe is incomplete.

But Butor, the most realistic of the new novelists, has also been the one most interested in form, the one whose language is the most complex and the freest in relation to its subject. Butor's first works were not nearly so radical as Robbe-Grillet's, because Butor was much less interested in breaking with the traditional framework of the novel than with dealing with specific subjects while still preserving a great deal of that framework. *Milan Passage*, for example, was an evocation of life in an apartment building in contemporary Paris. *L'emploi du temps* (1956, Allotment of Time) reconstructed the experiences of its narrator-hero in the town of Bleston, in which he still lives several months after the events described. *The Change*—noteworthy for the innovative use of the second-person point of view—was the story of a man who, while traveling by train from Paris to Rome to see his mistress, gradually reverses his decision to leave his wife, who lives in Paris; he thus also chooses between the two cities. In *Degrés* (1960, Degrees) a teacher of history and geography attempts to write a total description of an hour-long class held one Tuesday, October 12, 1954. The effort leads him to reconstruct not only the class but also his life, the life of the pupil whom he is particularly focusing on as he is speaking, the teaching staff, and so on.

In short, while he retained the traditional framework of the novel, Butor's aim in these works was to find an order (frequently symbolized by some kind of schedule) in a reality that seems to reject order in both time and space. Thus, the quest for order acknowledged the lack of order. The past resuscitated in the present is added to the past, or modifies it; the movement of consciousness and of the writing reacts on the object described; the event has to be described from multiple and contradictory viewpoints.

The novel as a quest, a re-search, for order could not end in anything other than failure, and the story of that failure is told in all these novels, in *Degrees* in particular. But Butor renounced the novel rather than the quest, and he who began by accepting what Robbe-Grillet rejected from the start was to contest far more. Indeed, one cannot use the term "novel" to describe Butor's more recent works, such as *Mobile* (1962, Mobile) and *Réseau aérien* (1962, Aerial Network), in both of which he superimposed images and assembled and dismantled linguistic structures. In these works time and space are described on the scale of the American continent, with countless variations on the events, which are out of phase because of the different time zones; Robbe-Grillet's narrative focus on an object was adopted in its fullest extension—the perspective of place (*Le génie du lieu* [1958, The Spirit of the Place] was the title of a collection of Butor's informal travel impressions).

Nor can the term "novel" be used to describe Butor's *Description de San Marco* (1963, Description of San Marco) or *6,810,000 litres d'eau par seconde* (1965, 6,810,000 Liters of Water per Second), in which pictures alternate with voices reading different texts (which come from classical literature or from someone's diary), forming something resembling a cantata or an opera. *Votre Faust* (1969, Your Faust), on which Butor collaborated with Henri Pousseur, *was* an opera. And his latest work was entitled *Dialogue avec 33 variations de Ludwig van Beethoven sur une valse de Diabelli* (1971, Dialogue with

33 Variations by Ludwig van Beethoven on a Waltz by Diabelli). The audience Butor addresses his works to has become more and more an audience of listeners (we hear tones and dissonant or harmonious voices) or of viewers (we see striking typographical arrangements) than of readers following the thread of a text by an abstract effort of the imagination. He has moved away not only from the novel but from literature, toward a synthesis hinted at in the composer Luciano Berio's *Omaggio a Joyce*, for example.

Butor has tried to make his style escape from any set pattern. It is almost impossible to speak of a characteristic Butor sentence structure. His sentences are either protracted or succinct, flowing or syncopated, as required by the subject and the psychological time response; they are less comparable to written communication than they are to parts of a musical score or a typographical construction. Butor, like the others, has ultimately given us structures to play with, and we are even invited to make our own choices, to use the elements provided—the scenario to be enacted or the happening to be pursued—to give our own performance. But Butor's game is quite different in spirt from that of the other new novelists because, in the arid landscape of contemporary questioning, his work has something of the "modernist" exaltation of the 1920s. His game is not so much a compensation—what remains in spite of all—as it is a gift of happy discovery in a world that is inexhaustible and continually renewed.

Claude Simon is the only one of the new novelists who has not written on the theory of the novel; the exception to this are the few pages of the preface to *Orion aveugle* (1970, Blind Orion), a short novel intended to be part of a collection entitled *Les sentiers de la création* (The Paths of Creation), whose specific aim will be to shed light on the creative process. Moreover, in this preface Simon merely said that the theory is entirely contained in the example, in the practice of writing. However, a few passages in his novels themselves suggest a theory. In *Le vent* (1957, The Wind), for example, he speaks of a "grammar without syntax." And in *Histoire* (1967, Story), he speaks of "those old, worn films, haphazardly cut and spliced, whole sections of which have been lost, with the result that from one frame to another, and without our knowing why, the bandit who just had the upper hand is lying on the floor dead or captured . . . scissors and glue replacing the director's careful narrative and restoring to the action its striking discontinuity." Indeed, this passage may be the best single definition of the technique of the *nouveau roman.*

Yet Simon's general reluctance to theorize tells us a great deal. He is by nature more of a novelist than any of the others. He is compelled by the need, if not to tell stories, at least to retrace or "restore"—to use the word that appears in the subtitle of *The Wind: Tentative de restitution d'un rétable baroque* (Attempt to Restore a Baroque Retable)—an imaginary or even an actual experience. For in Simon's work, unlike that of the others, there are not only key images but key events to which he returns again and again and on which he never tires of musing. And these events are sometimes taken from his own experiences, such as the Spanish civil war, evoked in *Le palace* (1962, The Palace), and the collapse of the French army in 1940, described in *La route des Flandres* (1960, The Flanders Road). As in the novels of Faulkner, who clearly served Simon as a model in his first novels,

The Wind and *L'herbe* (1958, The Grass), even in the stylistic mannerisms there is an obsession with an irreparable and secret past that has interfered with the flow of life; the novelist attempts to recapture it in order to understand what has happened and to reopen the wound.

Simon's style has neither the clarity of a descriptive factual account nor the flexibility of a recording of a voice, but rather the twisting, sidetracking insistence of a hesitant retrospection continually going over the same ground. In a way, each of his books can be considered a single sentence, somewhat as in Proust's novels. The voice of memory is the dominant voice and gives his work its epic tone. But the visual elements are very important, and his images burn with the intensity of an hallucinatory recollection. (This explains why Maurice Merleau-Ponty, a philosopher who has investigated human perception, has taken a particular interest in Simon.)

Simon's first works were very close to the traditional novel, but he has increasingly eliminated all traces of narrative continuity and the mediation of characters, and he has moved closer and closer to the manner of the *nouveau roman. Story*, although so titled by antiphrasis, still followed a pattern of events, in which the experiences of the narrator on one particular day are intermingled with those previously encountered by his uncle. But in *The Battle of Pharsalus* and in *Les corps conducteurs* (1971, Conductive Bodies), the narrative is almost completely disjointed and defies any retelling. Nevertheless, by reducing the novel's subject to a minimum, by adopting a framework so vague that anything can be fitted into it (*Conductive Bodies*, for example, is merely about a man on his way from one part of a large American city to another), Simon succeeded in establishing a continuity, a "conductibility," which is true to the spirit of the novel. Although *Conductive Bodies* is merely a series of associations, they have a forward movement and an unbreakable sequence. In Robbe-Grillet's work such associations are like juxtaposed slides, but Simon's associations have the motion, even if it is somewhat jerky, of a film. (He showed that he was aware that his goals were different from Robbe-Grillet's by abandoning the original, unsatisfactory title of *Conductive Bodies*, which was *Structures*.) Simon's works have power, an ever-free lyricism (reminiscent of Henry Miller), and a great vitality.

These four writers—Sarraute, Robbe-Grillet, Butor, Simon—despite their individuality, have been the chief representatives of a common quest. And although this quest has taken different forms, it started from assumptions that were close enough to allow us to speak of a movement. This group also includes Claude Ollier (born 1922). His *La mise en scène* (1958, The Staging) appeared around the same time as Robbe-Grillet's first books and offered, in the form of a journey through an imaginary continent, a completely "objectal" vision of things. In *Le maintien de l'ordre* (1961, The Maintenance of Order) Ollier presented a fantasia of the external world.

More important than Ollier has been Robert Pinget (born 1919), a very individual and complex writer. His first novels, such as *Graal flibuste* (1956, Buccaneering Grail), ironic and fanciful, showed a great verve for language and were based on no discernible preconceived theoretical position. Later, in *L'inquisitoire* (1962, The Inquisitory), Pinget moved closer to the narrative techniques of Robbe-Grillet. But in *Quelqu'un* (1965, Someone) and *Passacaille* (1969, Passacaglia) he turned away from strict observation to follow the movement of a speech refracted by different modes of listening, arbitrarily broken into until it becomes one with existence itself.

Many other similar writers could be mentioned, and their very abundance proves that, like the existentialist writers of yesterday, the writers of the *nouveau roman* do constitute a movement, if not a "school." Yet, considering the way the *nouveau roman* as a whole has been tending, we may well wonder what has become of the desire of these novelists to find a precise redefinition for the genre of fiction. Collages of images, symmetrical arrangements, and structural permutations have little to do with narrative movement, of which Beckett has still retained the essentials. We may admire a page chosen at random, but we do not feel at all compelled to read the next one immediately. The novel is in danger of becoming a prolix and basically inferior form of poetry. The writers of the avant-garde review *Tel Quel* have replied that it is becoming a "text."

Indeed, there is already a post-*nouveau roman*; the fact that one does not know whether to place Jean Ricardou's (born 1935) *L'observatoire de Cannes* (1961, The Cannes Observatory), for example, *in* or *after* the *nouveau roman* is a good illustration of the relationship between the *nouveau roman* and what has followed it, namely, textual literature, or rather textual writing, whose mouthpiece is the review *Tel Quel*. Ricardou's book pushed the primacy of description to its extreme limit, and at this limit "reality" takes on a very unreal aspect. But Ricardou insists that we not re-create, on the basis of this unreality, the suggestion of a human drama. When he said of Robbe-Grillet's *Jealousy* that it is less the "writing of an adventure than the adventure of writing," he was reproaching readers for misinterpreting it. But "less" is not the same thing as "not." Ricardou implicitly recognized that there is some justification for this misinterpretation in reading Robbe-Grillet. In each line of his own work Ricardou seems conscious of the need to avoid the slightest ambiguity. Seemingly subservient to the object, writing reveals the object's emptiness and establishes itself in the object's place.

This is also what the *nouveau roman* said—but sometimes forgot. Indeed, what separates the two movements, apart from a difference in chronology (there is a gap of ten years between dates of birth, and between first literary efforts), is a radicalization by the textual writers of the theoretical and collective nature of the quest of the new novelists. The newcomers have endeavored to be what their predecessors were thought to be, but hardly were. They have a desire for a group approach to theory, a desire to formulate jointly a doctrine fully corresponding to the conditions of the time. In this desire they are closer to the surrealist movement, many of whose features they share: internecine conflicts, excommunications, deviations and schisms, the polemical mood. But lacking the lyrical fervor of the surrealists, the textual writers present a vision that is cold, cerebral, and positivist. The group approach, insofar as it is something other than the emotional need for a community, clearly shows that, although literature is still their aim, writing is no longer regarded as personal expression. What is important can only be achieved jointly; in other words, they regard the practice of writing as a form of scientific knowledge and a means of political activity.

All this takes us a long way from the *nouveau roman*.

The new novelists willingly signed letters of political protest and aligned themselves with leftist movements, but
their work was not dictated by political imperatives. On
the other hand, if writing is transformed into a means of
action, the practitioners cannot do without an orthodoxy
or a political party. The writers of the *Tel Quel* school
may waver between Stalinism and Maoism, as the surrealists did between Stalinism and Trotskiism, but they
must in any event align themselves with the truth of a
power, or with the power of a truth. The predilection for
the novel as an art form, evident in their predecessors,
had no justification for the textual writers. All writing is
primarily a "text," whatever form it may take. The poetry
of Denis Roche (born 1937) is as characteristic of this
movement as is the fiction of Jean Thibaudeau (born
1935), Jean-Louis Baudry (born 1935), or Philippe Sollers
(born 1936). And, indeed, it is sometimes hard to see
what the difference is between what they label poems
and what they label novels.

Among the few writers of the past the textualists are
willing to include in their canon, Lautréamont (1846–
1870, pseudonym of Isidore Ducasse) and the Marquis
de Sade (1740–1814), Bataille and Artaud, are valued
more than Kafka or Joyce. And among contemporary
writers they consider the poet Francis Ponge (born 1899)
closer to them than Robbe-Grillet. We are thus witnessing a radicalization of the limited domain of the *nouveau
roman* and the extension of that limited domain into all
of literature, literature transformed into a unified field
of writing. And they identify their concept of writing
with revolutionary practice.

Yet neither *Tel Quel*, founded in 1960, nor its leading
figure, Philippe Sollers, took this extreme position at the

outset. The first novels of Sollers—*Une curieuse solitude* (1958, A Strange Solitude) and *Le parc* (1961, The Park)—later disavowed by him as "bourgeois literature," were sufficiently traditional to have gained Sollers the sponsorship of both Mauriac and Aragon. And the first issues of *Tel Quel*—in line with the most obvious sense of the title, ("as is") which is taken from a collection of essays by Valéry—gave literature a function of "representation" that implied a lack of moral and political commitment. Their aim was to accept what is, in other words, to express, to describe; and they approved of Robbe-Grillet because of his rejection of any final purpose or anthropomorphic significance. But by the same reversal that occurred in Robbe-Grillet, and which they were to take even further, they found very soon that this very expression is a fiction, a creation of writing. Reality must be extracted *from* writing, or rather, reality *is* the writing. More exactly, writing functions like a code and thus corresponds to a *"signifié"* (signified). But since the structuralists reject traditional notions of symbol and meaning, this "signified" is not to be regarded as the model of the signifier; the two—word and object—cannot be distinguished. There is but one "signified expressed scripturally" ("There is no break in substance between the book and the world," said Roland Barthes).

Thus, for the textual writers, since writing no longer reflects but *is* reality, it is an action, and, they claim, it must inevitably be a revolutionary action. On one level, the opposition between traditional literature and the new textual writing corresponds to the opposition between bourgeois order and revolutionary praxis. Traditional literature conveys a meaning and is readable; it is said to be an expression of the world. This is because it transmits a text written in advance and eschews action because it is there to protect and preserve. For the textual writers, to act is the opposite of to represent; and to act is to emit a "signifier" that projects—far ahead—a future "signified." Moreover, this kind of writing can only be "plural." For them, creation is not the act of one person only, seeking individuality of style. Thus, the textualists prefer the word "production" to the word "creation." Not only is narrative—which they regard as an individual myth—left behind; not only is there a disintegration of the boundaries separating the genres; the very concept of "writer" is brought into question. They claim that, deep down, through what has remained unsaid or through what has been unconsciously disclosed, literature has always been an anonymous text; it must now be so in full awareness.

Many arguments can be put forward in opposition to the textualists' theories, without going into all of their intricate and endlessly subtle defenses. One might well, for example, express surprise at their alignment with the Communist Party, the defender of a system in which literature is precisely the opposite of what the textual writers advocate, in which it has indeed ironically become the epitome of bourgeois art. But my purpose here is not to argue with the logic of the textualists. And it is only fair to say that the journal *Tel Quel* has become the most remarkable literary phenomenon of the present day. It has achieved such importance by linking literary theory with the major currents of contemporary philosophical and scientific thought, with psychoanalysis and modern linguistics as well as with Marxism and structuralism. In return, it has become a meeting place for some of the most important thinkers of the present, whether or not they are sympathetic to *Tel Quel's* cause: philosophers like Michel Foucault (born 1926) and Jacques Derrida (born 1932), psychoanalysts like Jacques Lacan (born 1901), Marxists like Louis Althusser (born 1918), semiologists like Roland Barthes, and scientists like Claude Lévi-Strauss (born 1908).

Although one must acknowledge the importance of the *Tel Quel* movement (and unlike the new novelists, the textualists clearly regard themselves as a movement), one can still regret that there is no other comparably powerful movement. Seen from the point of view of literary criticism, the program of the *Tel Quel* group is much more interesting than the examples, the theory is superior to the practice (with surrealism, the reverse was true). But the textualists reject the critic's prerogative of fitting their new practice into old literary categories, because they reject the old literary categories. If one expresses disappointment at finding that many of the writers are interchangeable or that many of the works are unreadable, he will be told that this is precisely what was intended. (They have even spoken of a "continuity of the unreadable.") This may be their intention, but the old categories can still be used so long as textual writing remains this side of the limit beyond which such categories are no longer valid. The interchangeability and unreadability are not such that one cannot, here and there, identify or prefer a particular writer. And because their political effectiveness has not yet been demonstrated, what else is there to fall back on but literary effectiveness?

From this standpoint, the work of Philippe Sollers has undoubtedly been the most outstanding of the group.

Drame (1965, Drama), as even its title suggests, has a gripping intensity concealed beneath the half-light and the whisperings midway between sleep and waking. *Nombres* (1968, Numbers) sparkles with a strange and sometimes magnificent abstract lyricism. Moreover, Sollers's theoretical and critical essays—*L'intermédiaire* (1963, The Intermediary), *La littérature et l'expérience des limites* (1965, Literature and the Experience of Limits)—have shown him to be the most subtle and vigorous mind in the movement. His turns of phrase frequently have a cutting edge and a quality of aggression that recall the Breton's surrealist manifestos.

The lyricism of Jean Thibaudeau in *Une cérémonie royale* (1960, A Royal Ceremony) and *Ouverture* (1966, Overture) has been more concrete, more direct than Sollers's. Jean-Pierre Faye's (born 1925) work is also distinct enough to be discussed as an individual accomplishment. Although at first inseparable from Sollers, even to the extent that Sollers joined him before the cameras when Faye was awarded the Prix Renaudot for *L'écluse* (1964, The Lock), as if the entire group were the prizewinner, Faye later broke with Sollers and founded the review *Change*. While this break had political implications, it was primarily prompted by the desire of Faye and his friends to maintain the contact between writing and a more immediate reality. His novels (*La cassure* [1961, The Break], *Battement* [1962, Beat]) are set in the specific contexts of current history (the situations in Berlin or Jerusalem); but at the same time they provide us with an interpretative "grid" revealing quasi-mathematical or "formalizable" groups and combinations, which correspond to the textualists' "signifieds."

All the young writers whose work is at all significant have had a common starting point. They realized that society and its literary expressions were outworn, and they felt that all meanings had become obscured, with the result that no meaning or value is possible without a complete break with the past. But, fortunately, some writers have still found it possible to react to these discoveries in a less abstruse way. J. M. G. Le Clézio (born 1940), in his first novel, *Le procès-verbal* (The Interrogation), which was published in 1963 when he was twenty-three, also reflected on the power of writing: "There was a sign, there will be a meaning." He rejected the concept of genre, saying, "Only one thing counts for me, that is the act of writing. The structures of the genres are weak." Le Clézio was clearly expressing what many others were saying at that time. But his tone even then was somewhat different. For Le Clézio, to write is to go as far as possible in a living relationship with the world, a world that is no longer the discourse of an alienating society written and spoken in advance, but the world in the sense of what we see, what surrounds us—from the galaxy to a blade of grass. Huge reversals of scale between the infinitely vast and the infinitely minute bring into question the situation of the individual, who is the intermediary. Hence the scene in *The Interrogation* in which a man fighting with a rat sees himself reduced to its size while the rat grows to his.

Le Clézio's power of imagination and language has enabled him to put himself in the place of each thing. Where others reduce the world to the object or the sign, he enlarges the world as much as possible, multiplying the focuses of a consciousness, of a "material ecstasy." He has the gift of metamorphosis, of communion; indeed, his *Terra amata* (1967, Terra Amata) tends toward a pantheistic lyricism reminiscent of Giono. Yet Le Clézio's work has in no way been a hymn without a discordant note; he also knows the sounds of rebellion and has denounced the death belt created by western urban civilization, as can be seen in *Haï* (1971, Hated).

But the most interesting aspect of Le Clézio's work is his ability to evoke those states of being in which we are unable to communicate and become enclosed in ourselves: toothaches, tiredness, the feeling of being cold (these are the themes of the stories in *La fièvre* [1965, Fever]). But the forward movement, the march— *L'homme qui marche* (The Man Who Marches) is the title of a story in *Fever*—makes it possible to find the rhythm again. Writing, for Le Clézio, is a march, the rhythm of life between cosmic death and human death, between physical death and the false life of civilization; it is impulse and affirmation. His language—torrential, violent, often magnificent but occasionally prolix and didactic—is the ideal vehicle for his imagination.

Is there any future for other approaches to literature, which, if not entirely uncommitted, are at least not merely satisfied to apply programs? And, more precisely, is there any future for the nonprogrammatic novel? It should be noted that, in spite of the evident disintegration of the genres, there still exists a basic resistance to a unification of all literature. In other words, whenever literature proceeds from an impulse rather than an intention, it approaches something resembling a genre.

The course of contemporary poetry has borne out the continuing validity of genre even more.

CONTEMPORARY POETRY: OLD MASTERS

Contemporary French poetry does not have the extensive sales of the novel, which remains the most popular genre with both the reading public and the literary juries. (From 1945 to 1960, the Nobel Prize was awarded five times to a French novelist, only once to a poet.) But because of political events, poetry between 1940 and 1950 did acquire an unaccustomed immediacy and an unusually wide audience.

Poetry, true poetry, has never been very popular in France: with a few exceptions, poets have not dealt with national concerns, and they have spoken in a difficult, terse language. Indeed, it would be impossible to reconstruct the history of France from its poetry. Even World War I left only echoes such as those found in Péguy and Apollinaire. But World War II, especially the French Resistance, produced a politically committed poetry that transformed or broadened already familiar voices and encouraged newcomers to address themselves to immediate concerns.

The poetry of the Resistance sought a language of communication, for it spoke about the world of common experience. Thus, poets seem to have been drawn toward anything that could reestablish the contact they had almost always failed to make previously, whether because of the purity of their form or because of their personal, confessional subjects. The Resistance poets reacted to experiences that confronted not only themselves but all of France, to events, scenes, and objects on which all eyes converged; they no longer strained after singularity. The pronoun "I" thus became less important than "we." Poets drew their inspiration from common feelings or sought to bear witness to the common fate of twentieth-century man. And the form of this poetry, whether it reverted to a more-or-less traditional style and verse form, or whether it adopted the simplicity of prose, was always designed for communication.

Soon after the war, however, French poetry began to be questioned by the very people involved in its creation. Poetry developed an anti-poetry, just as the novel did an anti-novel, and the theater an anti-theater. Before 1945, from Charles Baudelaire (1821–1867) to the surrealists, poetry had increasingly annexed areas of life that had earlier been judged unworthy of it. Although poetry seemed to be becoming more prosaic, it was paradoxically making these areas of life more poetic. ("You gave me mire, and I have made it gold," wrote Baudelaire.) Today, on the other hand, writers utilize elements that they refuse to call poetic. The poet no longer knows if he is a poet and is sometimes inclined to think he is not: to emphasize this doubt, Francis Ponge, for example, has called some of his writings *proêmes* (proems). In the extreme, a writer will write only texts that purposely defy classification by genre.

But this extreme has been less of a burden on poetry than on the novel. Poetry is less tempted by defeatism and silence. It is more innocent—more healthy, one might say. Is this because man needs to be able to express private experiences, needs a dimension that is inalienably poetic? Or is it because the universal destruction of a literature of expressivity is being delayed by gifted poets, who are turning out to be stronger and more numerous than French novelists? Whatever the answer, the period from 1945 to the present has been one of the finest in the history of French poetry.

Several important poets whose literary careers began well before 1940 reached full maturity or completed their work during the war years or shortly after—and in some cases adopted fresh approaches and reached a wider audience.

Between the two wars, surrealism was the most important movement. Still, André Breton, in his *Manifeste du surréalisme* (1924, Surrealist Manifesto), saluted as a master one poet who never belonged to the movement— Pierre Reverdy (1889–1960). Reverdy was some ten years older than his disciples, and his genius flowered extremely early. His first publications date from 1915, but he continued to write right up to his death. In addition two journal-like works that contained valuable revelations about his attitudes toward his art—*Le livre de mon bord* (1948, My Log Book) and *En vrac* (1956, Pell-Mell)— Reverdy continued to create very fine poems: those in his last major collection, *Main d'œuvre* (1949, Handiwork), which included poems from 1913 to 1949; and those in *Les libertés des mers* (1959, Freedoms of the Seas).

Critics are only now beginning to set a high enough value on Reverdy's poems, which are among the finest created by any writer of this century. Overshadowed by the brilliance of the surrealist movement, Reverdy was regarded between the wars as a mere precursor of surrealism and was too quickly seen, from a purely historical point of view, as an example of the so-called literary cubism of the period 1910–20. Rereading him today, however, we can see that he had little connection with the poetic theories of the early twentieth century. In Reverdy's poetry one can find a balanced objectivity recalling the experiments of Apollinaire and Max Jacob, an explosive force resulting from the liberation of the image, and the shock value of unusual metaphorical sequences (as in the surrealists). But these characteristics were all subsumed into a dramatic force that was entirely Reverdy's own.

Far from being receptive to the world's diversity, Reverdy preferred to express a fundamental relationship between the world and himself; and one can say that he simply rewrote the same poem time and time again. This poem contained hardly any adjectives, metaphors, or images; nouns were its most important elements, and verbs expressed actions rather than states of being. The protagonists in this "drama" are the objects the poem evokes in muted yet insistent tones. For, however briefly, a drama is enacted. Something *happens* at the juncture between life as it is lived, as it continuously flows by, and the world evading life's advances. The pulse of night and day, the sky adrift, the fleeting images of the wind, the clock ticking, the lamp that measures time, the roads, crossroads of night where the traveler's footfall echoes, faces turning away, the backs of people departing, doors and windows half opened and then slammed again— these key images are always images of flight, of transience, of time passing; and they are drawn in the language of the most simple experience.

Reverdy's poetry suggested neither the absolute dominance of the imagination over the mind nor the total subordination of man to objects; instead, it depicted man's movement among real objects and his painful confrontation with them. Reverdy's was a poetry of feeling, of the inner self, a dense crystallization of brief moments of experience.

Although after the outbreak of the war Jules Supervielle (1884–1960) wrote nothing as important as *Gravitations* (1925, Gravitations) or *Le forçat innocent* (1930, The Innocent Convict), his *Poèmes de la France malheureuse* (1941, Poems for Unhappy France) showed that he shared the wartime vogue for politically committed poetry. He later published the collections *Oublieuse mémoire* (1949, Forgetful Memory) and *L'escalier* (1956, The Staircase), as well as various plays, among which *Le voleur d'enfants* (1949, The Child Stealer) was outstanding. From his early *Les poèmes de l'humour triste* (1919, Poems of an Unhappy Mood) through his last collection, *Le corps tragique* (1959, The Tragic Body), the tone of Supervielle's poetry was altered by the varying literary landscapes it passed through. He displayed a modernism akin to Blaise Cendrars and Valéry Larbaud in *Débarcadère* (1922, Landing Stage), and to surrealism after that. But despite his having dedicated a poem to Lautréamont, Supervielle had no fundamental connection with the surrealists, who in turn ignored him.

Some of Supervielle's poetry was not unlike the early
work of Henri Michaux (born 1899)—fabular travels of
exploration through the inner recesses of mind and body,
a sort of coenesthetic dream voyage. And this vein was
part of Supervielle from the beginning to the end of his
career. But at the same time, his poetry contained elements of mythology and a feeling of being profoundly
in tune with the cosmos and with eternity. Whatever trig-
gered the inspiration—whether it was the body seen as
prison for the mind, the pampas, a bird, or a tree—
Supervielle's poetry possessed the lyricism of a continuous flow of song. In his odes, fables, elegies, epics, or
simple songs, the melodic line was always there to make
the poem immediately understandable.

Supervielle managed to give the most modern poetry
the transparency and simplicity of a familiar tale. The
reason for this was the continual presence of a discursive,
anecdotal thread: for Supervielle was a teller of tales, as
was shown by his stories and plays, which so resembled
his poetry. Images, myths, and shifts in emotions were
presented in ordered sequences. And whether he was telling a tale, enlarging on it, recounting the creation of the
world, or inventing the words of God to man or of man
to the unknown, Supervielle's meaning shone clearly
through his limpid language.

Pierre Jean Jouve (born 1887) struck out in many
more new directions in his poetry after the war than did
Supervielle. From the beginning, Jouve's poetry was dominated by forebodings of disaster; he wistfully longed for
"paradise lost," and, still more strikingly, he prophesied
doom. Jouve has always seen history as the embodiment
of an eternal drama, as in the collection *La Vierge de
Paris* (1946, Our Lady of Paris). The poem *La chute du*

ciel (The Sky Is Falling) strikingly combined details of present disaster (the ruins of bombed towns, the passerby "measuring out his cross upon the sidewalk") and the intuited struggle of supernatural forces. But Jouve's poetry, while kindled by the fire of contemporary experience, has also pursued its own path in spirit and form. His later collections—*Ode* (1951, Ode), *Langue* (1952, Language), *Lyrique* (1956, Lyric), and *Moires* (1962, Watered Silks)—in which he used a more rigorous, more harmonious form often very close to traditional versification, have evoked a more tranquil atmosphere, even when, as in his most recent collection, *Ténèbre* (1965, Darkness), his subject was the approach of death through illness.

Jouve has also added to his considerable achievements in narrative myths since the war with the fine tale *Aventure de Catherine Crachat* (1947, Adventure of Catherine Crachat), and in expository prose with essays like *Le Don Juan de Mozart* (1948, Mozart's Don Juan), *Wozzeck, ou le nouvel opéra* (1953, Wozzeck, or the New Opera), *Le tombeau de Baudelaire* (1958, The Tomb of Baudelaire), and the autobiographical reflections in *En miroir* (1954, In a Mirror).

Although the young Jouve was attracted for a while by unanimism, it was a Freudian awareness of the unconscious that enabled him to discover himself. He rejected, however, any connection with the surrealists, despite their passionate interest in psychoanalysis. For he did not believe, as they did, in automatic writing: his words were hard-won prizes, highly wrought crystallizations. And he has been interested not so much in opening the flood gates of the imagination as in finding, through the themes of love and death, an interpretation of life that could culminate in catharsis—a catharsis that both illuminates meaning and gives the poem its music. "To achieve a poetic language that justifies itself as song" was his initial ambition, although he has approached this goal more and more closely as he has passed from the tormented, strangled expression of *Sueur de sang* (1935, Sweat of Blood) to the musicality of his most recent collections.

This change of tone corresponded to an evolution in the poet's life. In *Sweat of Blood* Jouve abandoned himself to the demoniac, to the tangled, suffocating world of guilty sexuality; the image of original sin is stamped upon life like the face of Christ on St. Veronica's veil. Based on Christian remorse and the new science of dreams, this revelation of existence revolved around a few recurring symbols: eye, hair, penis, vagina, the "sweat of blood," the moisture of copulation. Jouve knew that a person can only overcome what one has accepted, and from the start he worked toward clarifying the obscure, disentangling the insoluble. Life and language moved together toward this solution.

Jouve's struggle has not ceased, nor his memory of the original darkness faded. Jouve's latest poems do not tell about man conquering death through the glory of the word, of the immortal memory of the world snatched up in an instant into eternity. On the contrary, they describe the poet's impulse to escape from darkness, seeking a light that continually evades his grasp. Day has dawned, but so, too, has the battle—the day's battle.

Jouve has condensed the alexandrine and has used the *verset* (a biblical verse form) in controlled patterns of musical expression: strophe, antistrophe, epode. But this music is full of harsh cries. His poetry is quite different from the surrealist's poetry of instant experience (that of sensory data or of automatic writing); in Jouve, poetry and experience are grounded in and justify each other. Each moment is the gauge, the measure of a life in progress. This poetry of time and toil has no facile charm to attract the reader; for its essence is not to be found in the places in which it glitters most brightly, but rather in the dark, laborious path of its progress and development.

Though of impressive breadth and variety, Jouve's work has been too hermetic, too difficult, and too frequently intractable to appeal to a wide audience. Nonetheless, he has greatly influenced such younger poets as Pierre Emmanuel (born 1916) and Yves Bonnefoy (born 1923), and he seems today to be one of the few modern writers who has fulfilled all the requirements of the word "poet."

The war and its aftermath saw even more development in the work of Jouve's contemporary, Saint-John Perse (born 1887, pseudonym of Alexis Léger). Between the publication of *Anabase* (1924, Anabasis) and *Exil* (1942, Exile), during most of which time he was secretary general of the French Foreign Office, he concerned himself exclusively with his official activities, not with poetry. He was admired by some important writers, including Proust and Breton, but his silence almost led to his being consigned to oblivion, especially since the general public had not heard of him at all.

In 1940 Saint-John Perse came to the United States to escape the Nazi occupation and began writing poetry again. His situation was strongly reflected in *Exile*, which is the poet's account of this experience.

And in *Vents* (1946, Winds) he evoked the great currents that destroy, set in ferment, and rebuild the world of men; Saint-John Perse bore witness to the great world-wide disaster during which he wrote the poem. *Amers* (1957, *Seamarks*) also related the loneliness of the poet on the coast of a foreign continent, dreaming of the beacons lighting up the shores of his own country, which he refused to return to. Despite its context, however, these poems were timelessly outside all particular literary and historical periods.

Saint-John Perse's early poems belonged to the climate of postsymbolism. The privileged, the rare, the precious, and the exotic characterized his first works. But his poetry, like that of Claudel, who used the *verset*, was cosmic poetry. It evoked and celebrated the earth in its elemental manifestations: snow, rain, wind, sea, and sunlight. What the poet perceived was eulogized; the liturgical unfolding of his *versets* was a ceremony in honor of the cosmos. Saint-John Perse took the entire universe in his grasp, and thereby went beyond symbolist subjectivity and, like all the poetry of his time, moved toward the concrete.

The subject of Saint-John Perse's poetry has not been sensory data alone. He has proclaimed the ancient alliance between man and the world, the time-honored meaning of history and culture. His wondering gratitude has been directed above all toward man's imprint upon the world and toward the saga of human civilization. His is not only a poetry of the cosmos but also an epic enumeration of the works of man, a poetry of memory as well as sensation. Indeed, the cosmic imagery is perhaps no more than a stage setting of changelessness and evanescence in which the human adventure—the epic poem's true subject—is carried on. Monuments lost in the sand, corroded bronzes at the bottom of the seas, traces of vanished roads, abandoned temples, dead languages, un-deciphered hieroglyphs, outworn trades, obsolete words, forgotten sciences—all are so many landmarks illumi-nated by the blaze of poetry, the eternal profile of the pillar standing among the ruins as a sign of victory for man and defeat for death.

Saint-John Perse's series of cosmological poems— *Pluies* (1944, Rains), *Neiges* (1944, Snows), *Winds, Sea-marks*—and even *Oiseaux* (1963, Birds) could suggest distinctions between various moments in time, the last collection coinciding with a final rejection of history. But one cannot attribute such a fixed progression of thought to Saint-John Perse. In *Chronique* (1960, Chronicle) he took up history again, and the very early *Eloges* (1911, Praises) was clearly cosmological.

In fact, although one must acknowledge his varying emphases, Saint-John Perse's poetry has been at once a poetry of human civilization and of nature; and if he has simplified his language, his methods have remained the same. With all its verve and provocative force, his poetry is able to control as much as it unleashes, to subdue these elements to rhythm, to rhetorical cadence, to the strict architecture of a language suited as much to the prose writer or chronicler as to the poet. His images communicate surprise, abruptness, shock; Saint-John Perse has combined symbolist glitter with the unusual elements of more recent developments in poetry. But he has firmly subordinated imagery to the structure of the poem; the imagery illuminates rather than dazzles, and it is as pre-cise as it is recondite. Saint-John Perse's poetry is a meet-ing point of opposite impulses and traditions, and, like classical verse, it can support a detailed explication; for each word, each image, is exactly justified, however much the *verset's* stately progress draws us on and enchants us.

Neither Reverdy, Supervielle, Jouve, nor Saint-John Perse belonged to the surrealist movement. They were of a previous generation; their origins lay elsewhere; their purposes were different. And, since World War II, there no longer is a surrealist movement, apart from certain tiny groups of no importance. But there has remained a state of mind created by surrealism, to which Louis Aragon, the poet who moved furthest from it, paid homage in *The Unfinished Novel.*

Éluard and Aragon became the two great popular poets of the Resistance by adopting communism (of a very national kind). But their passage from surrealism to communism was not so strange, for surrealism had sought an anonymous style. And is not political poetry anonymous poetry established on a firm basis? When Éluard quoted Lautréamont's statement, "Poetry shall be created by everyone," he invited people to forget, during the time of fervor, that poetry was a highly specialized profession.

Paul Éluard was not the most important figure in the surrealist movement, but he was certainly the greatest poet—and the only one who was exclusively a poet. He was also the one who wrote the most moving and lasting poems of the Resistance. His militant collections—*Au rendez-vous allemand* (1944, At the German Rendez-vous), *Poèmes politiques* (1948, Political Poems), and *Une leçon de morale* (1949, A Lesson on Morality)— contained a few poems that broke down the barrier between poetry and public and were on everyone's lips. This was especially true of *Liberté* (Liberty), but also of *Hommage à Gabriel Péri* (Homage to Gabriel Péri),

Critique de la poésie (A Critique of Poetry) and *Couvre feu* (Curfew).

But committed poetry for Éluard was never simply poetry of circumstance, a flash in the pan. If we read *Choix de poèmes* (Selected Poems), a selection chosen by Éluard himself in 1946, we can find the very early *Poèmes pour la paix* (Poems for Peace), which date from 1918; they tell of the joy of women reunited with their husbands home from the front. At the end of *La vie immédiate* (1932, Life at Close Quarters), there is a *Critique of Poetry* that prefigures the one in *At the German Rendezvous* and says the same thing: the happiness of men is more important than the words of poets. Even in Éluard's early poetry there was, mingled with the more personal vein, a humanitarian, social note, a theme present long before World War II and his conversion to communism. Alongside *Médieuses* (Médieuses) and *Les yeux fertiles* (The Fertile Eyes), poems of pure love written during the 1930s, *Chanson complète* (1939, Total Song) announced the coming tragedy and bore witness to its first victims. Poems like *La victoire de Guernica* (The Victory of Guernica) and *Les vainqueurs d'hier périront* (Yesterday's Victors Shall Perish) were the first of the kind of poem Éluard was to bring to fruition in *Liberty*.

This is not to say that Éluard's poetry did not develop. His early collections, such as *Mourir de ne pas mourir* (1924, Dying of Not Dying) and *Capitale de la douleur* (1926, Capital of Grief), focused on a private voice, enclosed in its inner space, face to face with its dreams, in a sort of half-light in which nothing can be heard but the heart beating. In his collections of poetry after 1940 the overall tone changed considerably, especially in the movement away from solitude and toward communion. But if there was an evolution, there were no ruptures. His loneliness was always a longing for communion; his night, a hope for day. In his most personal phase, in fact, Éluard's poetry was not so much a poetry of solitude as of love. His progress was not from solitude to communion, but rather from the couple to the collectivity. And in his last years he continued to write admirable love poems, such as those in *Le dur désir de durer* (1949, The Deep Desire to Endure).

What Éluard's private and public poetry had in common was their generosity, their bounty. Éluard was the poet of man's love for woman, because he celebrated the impulse not to remain enclosed inside oneself, but to open and hold out one's hand to others. And it was natural that a voice made for singing about happiness should find its own happiness insufficient.

Moreover, Éluard's evolution moved from shadow toward increasing light. His first lyrics rose out of a dreamlike darkness, a "song containing night." In his last collections, on the other hand, a cleansed and purified sky spreads above a sparkling world full of iridescent objects, birds' wings, cool springs, vibrant colors. The rainbow of the phenomenal world opens out. The lovely poem *Blason des fleurs et des fruits* (1941, Blazon of Flowers and Fruits), for example, was a catalogue of things perceived; its function was to "give them to be seen." But even here, Éluard revealed not so much a new departure as a natural development: in his earlier phase night moved toward day, and in his last period sensation and object had no meaning except insofar as they spoke to the human heart: the experience of "man bound to the universe," "the harmony of man and gold—an earth-bound gaze." Éluard quite unequivocally presented a lyrical experience in the traditional sense.

Indeed, Éluard was France's last great lyric poet, for his poetry saw in love the privileged path to understanding the world, and his mode of expression remained from first to last not merely images or metaphors but—better yet—pure song. His poems cling to our memory; they were among the last that we can easily learn "by heart."

It is now twenty years since Éluard died, and, although he reached a sizeable audience toward the end of his life, he is now viewed as somewhat remote. This is easily explicable, for he was in many ways closer to the tradition of Baudelaire and even of Paul Verlaine (1844–1896) than to more recent tendencies. More "modern" writers (Henri Michaux, Francis Ponge, Jacques Prévert [born 1900]) have denied the primacy of lyric poetry and have been unconcerned with the poem as *form*. Éluard was censured by Breton because he asserted the superiority of poetry over dreams, the superiority of the "arrangement in poem form" over a word-for-word transcription of the dream. And the most recent French poets, even though they no longer find their chief source of inspiration in dreams, do not organize their poems so much as they disorganize them! Yet, even if Éluard is currently out of favor, his place in literary history is assured.

As a surrealist, Louis Aragon was more a prose poet than a writer of verse. And as a communist in the 1930s he was much more important as the novelist of *The Good Neighborhoods* (1936) than as the poet of *Hourra l'Oural* (1934, Hurrah for the Urals). It was World War II, with its combination of patriotic fervor and revolutionary zeal, that brought Aragon the poet both his eminence and his audience. However, the patriotic, neoclassical, and popular poetry that Aragon wrote then resulted from an objective decision, a sort of program decided on, rather than from inner personal necessity. He wrote the kind of poetry that he would have liked to see others write.

Aragon's wartime poetry was simple poetry reflecting everyone's preoccupations, a lyricism poured into metrical molds that made it easy to memorize. This explains his use of the alexandrine; this also explains his rather curious defense of rhyme: "I say it is not true there can be no new rhymes in a new world" (*Rhyme in 1940*). And in his use of rhyme there was perhaps more dexterity than inspiration.

Constantly mingled with Aragon's political subject matter was an almost Petrarchan love motif: Elsa in *Les yeux d'Elsa* (1942, The Eyes of Elsa), like Bérénice in his novel *Aurélien*, established the myth of a beloved woman's face, which is also the face of a whole people. And Aragon's finest poems explored the theme of love. He did have difficulty in achieving candor and passion (or desire for passion), which his own nature and the very profusion of his talents almost disqualified him from feeling. Equally antagonistic to passion was the virtuosity that enabled him to try out any and every device of versification, from those of classicism and romanticism through the most modern styles. But the emotional sincerity that Aragon sought at first (and so often in vain) from the future, he later found in the past, in *The Unfinished Novel* and *The Rooms*, which fed on the emotions stimulated by memory.

Aragon's and Éluard's departures from surrealism eventually enabled them to attract a new audience. True enough, their postwar work reflects their surrealist experiments. Nevertheless, Aragon's realism and social conscience, his attempt to renew prosody, to write clear understandable popular poetry, were rejections of everything that surrealism had affirmed. To a lesser degree, the same is also true of Éluard—not only because of the politicizing of his poetry but also because of his own nature and the beauty of his melodic line.

André Breton, on the other hand, always identified himself with surrealism. Leader of the movement from its very beginnings, he was also the only one who remained faithful to its spirit to the end. Such fidelity naturally meant less development. But despite the fact that Breton's sources of inspiration were the same at all periods of his career, he nevertheless wrote important works after 1940. His great poems of the 1940s—*Fata Morgana* (1940, Fata Morgana), *Pleine marge* (1943, The Further Edge), *Les états généraux* (1947, The Estates General), *Ode à Charles Fourier* (1947, Ode to Charles Fourier)—had the same eloquence, the same luminosity, the same great metaphorical vitality as the poems of *Clair de terre* (1923, Earthlight). *Arcane 17* (1944, Arcanum 17) revealed the same style of poetic prose that had made his *Nadja* so extraordinary. And in his essays, restatements of the true surrealism, *La lampe dans l'horloge* (1948, The Lamp in the Clock) or *Flagrant délit* (1949, Caught in the Act), there was the same authoritarian zeal as before.

But although Breton's techniques and ideas did not change, his relationship to reality did—because the world had changed. The altered world caused adjustments in Breton's thinking and led to the appearance of a new tone compounded of bitterness and nostalgia. Breton was forced to admit his failure: surrealism, which had scorned literature and wanted to alter life, in the end altered literature without affecting the world. But Breton was determined not to recant. What could he do but take a fresh, if melancholy, grip on the past? His last publications were songs of disappointed hopes and missed chances. Breton began to look toward Charles Fourier and the social utopias of the nineteenth century, toward the Germans Heinrich von Kleist and Johann Hölderlin, toward Gérard de Nerval (1808–1855), toward the poetic dreams of the romantic period. Breton did not react to circumstances as Aragon and Éluard had, accepting the time he lived in and trying to keep in step with it. *Arcanum 17* is a work of "discommitment," if there is such a thing, in which the poet found in "personal ways of feeling" an antidote to the tragedies of history.

But Breton was physically detached from the Resistance by having emigrated to the United States. Although he certainly espoused and defended the Allied cause, particularly in his many radio broadcasts, he never gave the event itself the status and dignity of a source of poetic inspiration. There was no room, in his view, for nationalist and political enthusiasm: at the very most, one might take up a defensive position, so to speak, or fight to keep the damage to a minimum, but not to establish an absolute value. Breton shared none of the hopes characteristic of the immediate postwar period. He and his friends had called for a revolutionary transformation of society, but although his colleagues seemed to be content with the directives of "strange comrade Stalin," Breton utterly rejected orthodox communism. His friendship with Trotski was essentially similar to his admiration for Fourier— a kind of nostalgia.

Like his friends, Breton had once hoped for destruction—the destruction of a society, of a culture, of a Europe whose "defeatists" they claimed to be. But he began to perceive not only that no improvement had come about in the world but that such changes as had occurred tended to discourage men from wanting further change. We had desired the end of the world—he said in *The Lamp in the Clock*, written just after the first atomic explosion—and now the end of the world stares us in the face, but "we want nothing more to do with it." For it was the world of history that man should have destroyed, but now history may destroy the world of man. It is easy to understand why Sartre wrote that Breton was an "exile in our midst" at a time when literature was committing itself to political optimism. Breton disdained any political stance that did not incarnate an absolute, and he was also a clear-sighted enough observer to see how treacherous were the paths to which others had blindly committed themselves.

From a literary point of view, Breton is closer to more recent tendencies, and Philippe Sollers has often cited him. But although the group around the review *Tel Quel* has borrowed from Breton the notion of literature as a unified field of activity—the idea that writing must not be the mode of expression of a finite and limited man but rather an activity directed toward totality—there is a great distance between Breton's notions of intuition and poetic necessity and *Tel Quel's* theoretical concerns. The textualists have attempted to integrate the chief contemporary theoretical disciplines; and they have suspected poetry of being invented by, and in league with, the bourgeoisie. Whatever he wrote, Breton was a poet, by virtue of the imagery, the sense of discovery, the thrill of life that accompanied his every word. Whether his mood was nostalgic or excited, whether he was rejecting or asserting, his work was still a sublime example of poetry as an attitude toward life.

Breton was surrounded to the end by the remnants of the surrealist group, and even after his death the group kept going, along with its successive reviews: *Bief, Le surréalisme même, La brèche,* and others. But no important new works resulted; the journals had to struggle to survive; the demonstrations that the group organized had a prehistoric flavor. Breton himself, toward the end of his life, was tempted to wind up the movement; the few interesting writers (such as Julien Gracq) who were associated with its last gasps, were not activists but rather nostalgic admirers of a past whose splendors they themselves had not known. What mainly remains today of surrealism is its history.

To this history, which is similarly the history of dadaism, also belong Tristan Tzara (1896–1963), Philippe Soupault, and Benjamin Péret (1899–1959). But what they produced after the war was considerably less important than their earlier work. At most, they played a part in the literary conflicts of the time: Péret, faithful to André Breton to the end, attacked in *Le déshonneur des poètes* (1945, The Poets' Shame) the patriotic, "propagandist" litanies of Aragon, Éluard, and Emmanuel. In reply to Péret, Tristan Tzara in *Le surréalisme et l'après guerre* (1947, Surrealism and the Postwar World), diagnosed the death of that movement: because surrealism had wanted to be outside the world, it could no longer find a place in the "circuit of ideas."

But this was mere pamphleteering. Robert Desnos (1900–1945), on the other hand, was on the verge of finding a new vein, if one can judge by the wartime poems such as *Fortunes* (1942, Fortunes), which had a simple, tightly strung lyricism. But he died in 1945, a few days after he was freed from a concentration camp.

One 1930s group related to surrealism was made up of writers connected with the review *Le grand jeu*. They developed surrealism's "occultist" side; but in opposition to surrealist dogmatism they proclaimed that spiritual experiences could not be precisely formulated. Among them, Roger Vailland was to take up postwar political positions similar to those of Tristan Tzara and become a committed writer. René Daumal (1908–1944) was by far the most important poet in this occultist group. He has won an increasing following through posthumous publications, especially through *Mont-Analogue* (1952, Mount Analogue), which has a preface by André Rolland de Renéville (born 1903). *Mount Analogue* strikingly recounts the myth of a voyage in search of an invisible world—a voyage that ends in death. Also important in this group was Roger-Gilbert Lecomte (born 1909), whose manifesto in the first issue of *Le grand jeu* ("We do not wish to write; we let ourselves be written") seems to have anticipated more recent theories, although Lecomte was speaking of "lived" experience and enthusiasm rather than analytical intelligence.

No writer has recently received more posthumous attention than has Antonin Artaud. The cult of Artaud, who died in 1948, dates only from the last ten years. In 1947 Artaud's speech of self-justification and self-criticism before a large audience in the presence of Gide, Breton, and Camus, produced a very uneasy atmosphere: Artaud seemed a sacrificial victim, not the "exemplar" he was to become.

Artaud left hardly more than the shreds and tatters of

a literary creation—or rather of his *refusal* to create. Yet the radiation from these fragments eclipses the carefully constructed and widely celebrated works of many other writers. Artaud appeared suddenly out of limbo, and he seems to have been the precursor and discoverer of all that now most concerns and disturbs us.

After the war Artaud published very important works, such as *Au pays des Tarahumaras* (1945, In the Land of the Tarahumaras), *Lettres de Rodez* (1946, Letters from Rodez), *Artaud le Mômo* (1947, Artaud the Bogieman), *Van Gogh, le suicidé de la societé* (1947, Van Gogh: Society's Suicide). But his immediacy is not to be explained by the fact that his last works were deeper and richer; the current enthusiasm for Artaud includes not only these more recent works but a rediscovery of his prewar writings, such as *L'ombilic des limbes* (1925, Umbilical Limbo); his meditations on the theater, *Le théâtre et son double* (1938, The Theater and Its Double); his experiments in tragedy, *Les Cenci* (1935, The Cenci), *Héliogabale* (1935, Heliogabalus)—in short, Artaud's entire œuvre.

Artaud's popularity may seem strange, for he was, as well as a genius, also a pathological case: a powerful enemy within himself separated him from himself, deprived him of speech, imprisoned him. Reading his works, we sometimes sense the wind of madness, with its accompanying deprivation of free will. But Artaud was able to make his sick obsessions the means to a revelation that involves us: and he even makes us question our customary policy of locking away the insane, by castigating the policy as social hypocrisy designed to protect us from our fear of recognizing ourselves in them.

By forcing us outside our usual reassuring boundaries, Artaud proves to us that we also inhabit those dangerous regions beyond all frontiers. In his ravaged body, his stammering, inconsequential phrases, we suddenly recognize the truth, the only truth. Artaud is the hero, or rather anti-hero, of a literature that has nothing whatever to do with escapism: what justifies literature is truth itself, not the creation of an opus or an escape to the "beautiful object."

In 1922 Jacques Rivière, editor of the *Nouvelle revue française*, rejected the poems Artaud had just submitted, complaining that they were shapeless. Artaud in reply expressed his contempt for the "Vermeer of Delft side of poetry." In the 1920s people agreed with Rivière, but today many think Artaud is right. And compared to Artaud, surrealism itself looks like an outburst of lyrical euphoria that suffers from a certain "Vermeer of Delft" side. The truth revealed and proclaimed by Artaud is life seen as evil and inadequate, seen also as an intensity of rebellion, ecstasy, and paroxysm.

Artaud consistently rejected the idea of literature as a fictitious and distanced version of life. He sought desperately for a word–gesture—a word–cry in his poems, a word–action in a theater that would no longer be a spectacle played by actors for an audience but a ceremony or a happening lived and shared. From Artaud, from his thought and his theatrical experiments, comes today's anti-theater and the audience participation that has succeeded Brecht's anti-theater of alienation—all the tendencies, in fact, that seek to raise art to the level of life, even at the risk of destroying art.

6

CONTEMPORARY POETRY: NEW MASTERS AND NEW PROSPECTS

After World War II the climate for French poetry was favorable: there were many poetry magazines, brilliant but unfortunately short-lived, such as Pierre Segher's *Poésie; Confluences*, founded in Lyon by René Tavernier and subsequently edited in Paris by René Bertelé; and, most notable of all, *Fontaine*, which appeared first in Algiers, then in Paris under the direction of Max-Pol Fouchet. These magazines provided great variety. Some poets spoke in a more-or-less traditional lyric voice, others attempted epic mythmaking, and still others adopted rhetorical or realistic approaches.

Lyricism cannot be defined simply. It is a framework for a wide range of subjective approaches; the poets classified as "lyric" are often very different from each other. They may find inspiration in events or in human relationships; they may be weavers of sound patterns—effusive or elliptical. But although they can be differentiated by subject, theme, or style, they can be identified as lyric because they overlap, they mingle, all these elements. Lyricism is a link between an individual consciousness and the world. It needs the resources of imagery and music. Even in the midst of grief or rebellion, lyricism is a state of exaltation; it has always remained a song in which existence is justified by being transformed into poetry. Lyricism can be recognized by the optimistic view it takes of poetic diction, by its enthusiasm for language.

Michel Leiris's poetry can unquestionably be called lyric. Before gaining a reputation principally for his autobiographical *The Rules of the Game*, he wrote the important collection of poems *Haut mal* (1943, Epilepsy), which contained the beautiful and eloquent *La néréide de la Mer Rouge* (The Nereid of the Red Sea) and *Abanico para los toros* (the Spanish title means "fan for bulls"), a poem-sequence about bullfighting that revealed both an extraordinarily precise vision and a great dramatic intensity.

Henri Thomas (born 1912) has also written both poetry and prose. In the poems in *Travaux d'aveugle* (1941, Works of a Blind Man) and *Le monde absent* (1947, The Absent World) he was able to alternate between the most moving lyricism and the most offhand humor. Sometimes unsure of his own voice, and consequently constantly tempted to alter his metrics and tone, Thomas has succeeded most often through a winning grace and spontaneity that evokes Verlaine.

Jean Cayrol is now better known as a novelist. But he first attracted attention for the lyric poems of *Les phénomènes célestes* (1939, Celestial phenomena) and *L'âge d'or* (1939, The Golden Age).

Jean Tardieu (born 1903) has divided his efforts between poetry and drama. His main collections of poems have been *Accents* (1939, Accents), *Le témoin invisible* (1943, The Unseen Witness), *Monsieur Monsieur* (1951, Mister Mister), *Figures* (1944, Figures), and *Une voix sans personne* (1954, A Voice without an Owner). Tardieu has combined a keen intelligence with a genuine feeling for classical versification to create an interpretation of the universe reminiscent of German romanticism (it is not coincidental that Tardieu has magnificently translated Hölderlin). In each poem Tardieu has sought to express, in rigorous and harmonious form, the confused awareness of a moment when the secret pattern of life and the world can be half-guessed at. The poet seeks to "apply to the visible world the precise and moving lucidity of dream and to restore to the most immediate reality its character as evidence of the supernatural." Tardieu's lyricism has breadth, depth, and brilliance. His poetry has also displayed irony and parody, especially in *Mister Mister*; but these tendencies found their true focus in Tardieu's plays.

André Frénaud (born 1907) has limited his literary activity to poetry. His work has been marked by sheer abundance and epic vigor. It is notable for its purity and spontaneity, profusion without bombast, brilliance without affectation—sharp and glittering as a blade. Frénaud is both profuse and untidy, but his untidiness is a virtue, for the level monotone of his classical versification never lulls us to sleep and the lines strike home to the heart; *La plainte du Roi Mage* (1943, Complaint of One of the Three Kings) has been his only example of standard verse form. Nonetheless, amidst the glitter of broken images, an alexandrine as taut as a bowstring often stands out firm and pure. But Frénaud takes care not to organize his poem down to the last word.

Because of his concision, profusion, fine disorder, the discontinuity of modernism intermingled with a classical fluency; because of his use of the Rhenish legend as background for the poems of captivity, such as *Poèmes de Brandebourg* (1947, Poems of Brandenburg); and because of his mingling of anecdotes, jottings as simple as a newspaper headline, and lyrical solemnity—because of all this Frénaud evokes Apollinaire. Frénaud's finest poems (many of which are his most recent)—*Poèmes de dessous le plancher* (1949, Poems from under the Floorboards), *Passage de la visitation*, (1956, Passage of the Visitation) and *Il n'y a pas de paradis* (1962, There Is No Paradise)—have a tragic discordancy, a nakedness shot through with sudden flashes which give one glimpses of his most private voice.

Philippe Jaccottet (born 1925) belongs to a more recent generation. He has been at his best perhaps in poetic prose rather than in his verse. His prose accomplishments include *Paysages pour figures absentes* (1970, Landscapes for Absent Figures) and translations of Leopardi and Musil. Jaccottet's work leads toward silence, toward the unsayable experienced as indestructible, expressed in distinct, dense, long pent-up voices, which mingle cadence and image in nostalgic autumn colors, as in *L'effraie* (1954, The Barn Owl) and *Airs* (1967, Airs). His work echoes both the French symbolist poets (and even, in its simplicity, Francis Jammes [1868–1938]) and the rich harmonies of Rilke, although in Jaccottet they are muted, austere, and extremely delicate.

Lebanon-born Georges Schehadé (born 1910), who has written a number of plays including the delightful *Monsieur Bob'le* (1951, Mr. Bob'le), clearly belongs to the lyric tradition. His poetry has been outstanding for its innocence and purity. His words shine with a dewlike freshness, but his simple—even naïve at times—graceful, and amusing poetry can also turn iron-hard and give glimpses of true profundity.

The lyricism of Aimé Césaire (born 1913), both a dramatist and a poet, shows epic strength and abundance in *Les armes miraculeuses* (1946, The Miraculous Weapons) and *Cahier d'un retour au pays natal* (1947, Diary of a Return to the Native Land). Césaire, a native of Martinique, is the first great black poet to write in French, and in return for what French culture (particularly surrealism) has given him, he has enriched French literature with a portrait of a new sensibility and of a new humanity. In his violence and verbal richness, one can glimpse the presence of a luxuriant volcanic land, as well as a spirit of revolt born of the conditions in which the black man finds himself. Césaire's verse has a jazz-like contrapuntality and drive.

But René Char, more than anyone else, today most brilliantly and masterfully embodies the lyrical impulse in poetry. Char's poetry best illustrates the essence of the poem, as Maurice Blanchot said, echoing Heidegger's evaluation of Hölderlin. Although he was associated with the second wave of surrealists, and his first works were published before the war—*Ralentir travaux* (1930, Slowing Down Work), *Le marteau sans maître* (1934, The Masterless Hammer)—Char found his true voice only after 1945. *Feuillets d'Hypnos* (1946, Leaves of Hypnos) was a verse diary of Char's combat action as a leader of the Maquis in Provence. *Leaves of Hypnos* overshadowed all other committed poetry because of its direct narration of scenes actually experienced. For instance, the poet witnesses the execution of one of his comrades and is powerless to intervene because the village in which this happens must be saved at all costs. There is no propaganda in *Leaves of Hypnos,* no political blandishment, but rather a morality, an affirmation of courage and comradeship, with no illusions and no program for the future.

The reserved, dense, often aphoristic lyricism of Char was quite unlike the melodious effusiveness of Éluard and Aragon. But although his poetry has always contained a thread of reference to the world of history, the collections *Le poème pulverisé* (1947, The Pulverized Poem), *Fureur et mystère* (1948, Frenzy and Mystery), *Recherche de la base et du sommet* (1955, Research Fundamental and Supreme), *La parole en archipel* (1962, Words in Archipelago), not to mention his plays, among which *Le soleil des eaux* (1949, The Water Sun) was especially notable, have made it clear that Char's poetry is very far from the literature of political commitment. His experience is lyrical. He has been concerned with what is sacred in the universe, with a mysterious relationship between human order and cosmic sensations, always going beyond any possible definition of its meaning.

Char has confined his poetry to experience, and has entrusted this experience to the fullness and perfection of form; and he accepts language itself. Whereas surrealism tended toward liberation, toward a dislocation of the linguistic mechanism, Char has condensed the richest experience into the hardest and most explosive language.

He has often ended up with maxims like those of Heraclitus, subsuming contradictions in the unity of a single tension. Imagery and metaphor (which have not always avoided preciosity; a meadow, for instance, is "day's watchcase") have been important elements in his poetry. But he uses them to create a passing glow, a flash of light rather than an object intended to be looked at. Like Char's aphorisms, his imagery and metaphors constitute a kind of gesture, a form of energy.

By condensing language, reducing it to the fundamental nuclei of its energy, Char isolates upon a page a number of atoms, so to speak, whose explosion will set off a chain reaction. His poetry sparks off and instigates much more than it actually relates; its unity is not that of a unifying consciousness but of a gesture that initiates. The tension maintaining the elements of language in violent equilibrium is that of a force coursing through life and opening up the future. The world's images glitter and glimmer like flint kindling the tinder of space. But this is a fire lit, rather than contained, by the poem. It gives one the taste and strength for life. The taste for life subsumes both the return toward primal innocence and a virile acceptance of life as it is. All times, like all contradictions, are fused: "Speech, storm, ice, and fire shall end by forming a common frost." Is this a prophecy or the reminiscence of a golden age? Neither. For past and future vanish in poetry's eternal present, in the golden moment of the poet's gaze riveted upon the world.

The postwar period saw some experiments that were in radical opposition to the surrealist and modernist modes of discontinuity. These writers required the poem to have unity; they asked it to follow an inner unifying logic, to become the narrative of a myth. Jouve was a major influence; but it is easy to understand why the postwar climate in general was favorable. The war had produced a world of absurdity that demanded description and interpretation at the highest level. Through the epic tradition, these writers hoped to find a meaning and a consistent form, to give answers to man's bewilderment, and to aid readers lost amidst so much obscure and disjointed poetry. Thus, these writers—especially Pierre Emmanuel (born 1916) and Patrice de La Tour du Pin —had nostalgia for the great eras of myth and religion.

Pierre Emmanuel, although influenced by Jouve, decisively transformed Jouve's approach from the start: the material was clarified, became more discursive. The qualities of the collection *Tombeau d'Orphée* (1941, Orpheus' Tomb)—a lofty, solemn eloquence; forceful images; maturity of forms—were surprising coming from a man of twenty-five. Painted in the colors of disaster, these poems seemed the opposite of escapism; they seemed to bear witness to the times.

Emmanuel's *Combats avec tes défenseurs* (1942, Combats with Your Defenders) was salutary and health-giving, uplifted by courage and hope; and the time was right. But it was not limited by circumstance: Emmanuel interpreted events and appearances according to a secret inner pattern, presupposing a vision and interpretation of the world. It was also an attempt to go beyond hermeticism, discontinuity, idiosyncracy by returning to the continuity of the narrative and descriptive poem, and to Greek and biblical mythology.

But can poetry step back in time like this without exposing itself to grave risks? Is it possible to create a poetry that can both interpret the universe and be universally understood? No single poet can do this. There would have to have been a group and an era whose natural mode of expression was poetry. Without this kind of support, such poetry is in danger of looking like an artificial re-creation. Moreover, even if the poem's meaning is supposed to be accessible to everyone, it cannot be openly presented: the meaning depends on the poem's inner logic; it is concealed by the language of the poem and is the jewel in the casket, the "image in the carpet." We have to work through the form to grasp it, and the form may then seem an empty envelope: in any case, the fusion of language is not achieved. These faults have been evident in Emmanuel's postwar work, such as *Babel* (1952, Babel) and *Jacob* (1970, Jacob). But an earlier collection, *Cantos* (1943, Cantos)—containing brief, dense, incantatory poems whose movement resembles song—revealed a quite different and unexpected Emmanuel, rapid and forceful.

The poetry of Patrice de La Tour du Pin (born 1911), although without patriotic inspiration, is not unlike Emmanuel's. There is the same striving for a metaphysical significance, the same struggle to create the organic poem, the great poetic composition, the same partial reinstatement of classical versification. La Tour du Pin's first poem, *Les enfants de septembre* (1932, September's Children), published in the *Nouvelle revue française* aroused great hopes. But La Tour du Pin turned his back on early success and went into retirement. Only in 1946 did he reemerge from this long silence, with a book six hundred pages long, *Une somme de poésie* (A Sum of Poetry), the first volume of projected work that is to be constructed according to a unified plan. La Tour du Pin's art is like that of cathedral building, or like the spiritual architecture of the Summa Theologica and of the Divine Comedy.

But there is perhaps an even greater distance in La Tour du Pin between ambition and achievement than there is in Emmanuel. Not that La Tour du Pin is not a poet. He has an individual voice, a personal mythology and a vision: his muted, hesitant song evokes a landscape of mists, marshes, and woodlands above which birds swoop and cry. But these qualities were present in the short *September's Children*, which still remains his finest poem. In A *Sum of Poetry* La Tour du Pin was not able to offer the sustained eloquence that great organic poetry requires, even supposing that such poetry were possible today. One could say that La Tour du Pin is an intimate, minor lyric poet who tries to speak like Vergil and Dante or like the Victor Hugo (1802–1885) of *La fin de Satan* (1886, The End of Satan), but whose voice is that of Verlaine or Jammes.

The spirit of Jean Grosjean's (born 1912) work— *Terre du Temps* (1946, Earth of Time), *Hypostases* (1950, Hypostases), *Majestés et passants* (1956, Majesties and Passersby)—can be likened to that of Emmanuel and La Tour du Pin. But Grosjean's form is very personal. *Majesties and Passersby*, for instance, is a single continuous poem whose meaning no one fragment can convey; for it is a series of dialogues in which biblical events and symbols bring about a confrontation between strong and weak, mortal and immortal. The poem's language has to conform to the needs of this dialogue: it seeks an explanation, and every line answers a previous line and provokes a reply, accuses or justifies. In other words, the poem's language depends upon its ability to last, to continue and to be re-created out of itself at every instant. The result is a sort of elliptical, fitful eloquence, a rhythmic lightness blended with a biblical solemnity.

Other poets' works, which were displays of language, plays on words, and rhetoric, were certainly more modern. The best example of this kind of poetry was the work of Jacques Audiberti (1899–1965). His eloquence found expression in his novels too (*Carnage* [1942, Carnage], followed by a whole brilliant series) and in the drama, which imposed restraints and thereby probably enabled him to do his finest work. *Le mal court* (1947, Evil Is in the Air) was a considerable success. Though in his later years he neglected poetry in the strict sense, Audiberti will still be remembered for the poems of *L'empire et la trappe* (1930, The Empire and the Monastery), *Race des hommes* (1937, Human Race) and *Des tonnes de semence* (1941, Tons of Seed).

Moreover, for Audiberti, fiction, drama, and poetry were all part of a single enterprise, which he described in his manifesto *La nouvelle origine* (1942, The New Beginning), which celebrated the poet as pure verbal technician and also drew on the romantic ideal of the poet as divine creator: "The poet shall not graft the world onto paper, or plagiarize it, or photograph it. He will make it positively, as if he himself, the poet, were the creator." Audiberti's remarkably rich, impetuous torrent of words adopted all the rhythms and forms of verse. He excelled both in lyric and epic modes, and both for him were primarily a flow of words, a rhetorical mold. His realm was not inhabited by feelings, images, or ideas, but by words, above all by their organizing forms. Yet his poetry was a compendium not only of versification and rhetoric but also of history, for in it the baroque, classicism, and romanticism meet in a brilliant and entertaining brew.

A newer current in poetry is one that can roughly be called "realistic." It has been characterized by a critical attitude, or an irreverence, toward poetry itself. In this anti-poetry the writer has sought, through either subject matter or language, to use jarring forms and materials. Is this to make the domain of poetry limitless? Or is it to show that nothing is poetic? A reply to these questions must depend upon one's own temperament.

Jean Follain (1903–1970), an important minor poet, created realistic poetry cunningly but unaggressively. From *La main chaude* (1933, Blind Man's Buff), his first collection, to the more recent *Exister* (1947, Existing), *Territoires* (1953, Territories), and *D'après tout* (1967, According to Everything), Follain continually affirmed his individual voice. His Norman temperament made him suspicious of great lyrical outbursts of eloquence, and of intellectualism. He wrote short poems whose tone is never lofty or expansive, whose imagery is striking, but simple, borrowed from the most everyday reality; there is a rustic and provincial quality, a taste for still life, for draper's shops, for peasant lace bonnets and the village school.

Follain was usually content to let his gaze follow the suggestion of simple gestures and then capture them as if in slow motion. Everything, even the brevity of his texts, makes one think of a miniaturist. And yet, beneath the surface of his poetry lurks a hidden drama: grandeur, pathos, a deep sense of the mystery of existence, of the eternal order that encompasses the most commonplace gestures and objects. Follain's entire art consisted of making this mystery brush against the surface of reality. Each poem is thus like a tarot card with the vivid colors of a poster; if we turn it over, we can see the disquieting face of fate.

Although his methods have been different, Eugène Guillevic's (born 1907) efforts have been much on the same order as Follain's. In collections like *Terraqué* (1942, Terraqueous), *Carnac* (1961, Carnac), *Paroi* (1970, Partition), he offered an abrupt, rugged, brutal poetry. Unlike Follain, Guillevic has shunned all melodic attractiveness: his poems are ungraceful successions of short, gritty, guttural words. His style clearly constituted a step beyond Follain in this "criticism" of poetry.

A poem by Guillevic is not a rhetorical exposition; it is speech harshly uttered, and his best poems strike home like bullets. The elements that compose these tiny compact explosive masses are the simplest and most concrete of things: the titles of *Choses* (Things) and *Faits divers* (News in Brief), two parts of *Terraqueous*, are indicative. Bench, bowl, wardrobe, tree, rock, the motions of workmen, of love, of death, of ordinary life, constitute Guillevic's universe.

But from Guillevic's objects and gestures there emanates a disquieting light. By juxtaposing them, by naming them in a solemn incantatory way, by spreading emptiness around them, by isolating an object that normally appears in the reassuring context of other objects, Guillevic informs all he touches with an unfamiliar magic. Even silence is compelled to listen. And then we hear an ancient, drowsy speech, crystallized in the knots in the wood or the shelves of a wardrobe. Long-effaced signs of man rise back to the surface. Without legend or myth or recourse to an imaginary world, Guillevic has revived a disturbing animism.

For Guillevic, realism is thus a detour rather than an end in itself. His purpose is to force objects to tell what they know of man. The violence, the impulse to rebel, the strangled cry, the clenched fists—what meaning could they have if they had no bearing on man? Man is the final purpose, the text hidden within this poetry of still life. In *Fractures* (1947, Fractures), Guillevic more openly admitted his purpose; the poem is a martyrology of dead Resistance fighters, the very model of a committed poem.

Jacques Prévert has also belonged to this school of realistic reappraisal, with its deflation of language and its simple inspiration. But Prévert's career has been very special, not least on account of his great popular success: *Paroles* (1946, Words), which included both old and new poems by Prévert, is the only collection of poems whose sales have equaled or exceeded that of a best-selling novel. Counting paperback editions, *Words* sold a million copies in its first twenty years. This success was partly due to the fact that Prévert already had a vast audience through his screenplays for such films as *Le jour se lève* and *Les enfants du paradis*. Nonetheless, he is the one poet who will have a place in the history of literature and in popular culture.

What was so different about *Words* and the collections that followed it: *Spectacle* (1951, Show), *La pluie et le beau temps* (1955, Rain and Fine Weather), *Fatras*

(1956, Hodge-Podge)? A diction rather than a style—
the shorthand of a nonchalant improvisation. And the
subject matter? The air and the images of the street;
stories about anyone, principally love stories, but a love
emptied of drama and often equated with pleasure.

Although this sounds more like song writing than
poetry, it soon becomes obvious that literature, in the
best sense of the word, has its share here as well. However spontaneous Prévert's verve may be, it develops into
an organized, and extraordinary instrument for catching
words and knocking them off course. He obtains irre-
sistible effects from collages that recall the surrealists'
plays on words, and spoonerisms that come from a much
earlier tradition in French literature. However innocent
this poetry may be, it is nonetheless animated by a criticism, a reappraisal of poetry; and no doubt Prévert's
irreverence, his hostility to social, religious, and national
myths, his denunciation of idols and privileges all express
an old anarchistic tradition, which has also inspired many
French popular singers.

But Prévert's satirization of society is also a satirization
of society's language, of its cliches and sententious maxims. This satire is not designed to bring down the final
curtain, but rather to encourage a change in setting.
Prévert has rejected the language of conventional pro-
priety. He delights in a fresh, rejuvenated language, and
he has realized its potentials: he has brilliantly handled
not only epigrams and profanities, the humor of repartee,
the banter of slang, but also the tender voice of ballads
and songs.

What a distance there is between the vivacious simplicity of Prévert and the very different simplicity of

Francis Ponge, whose poetry starts with the object itself and ends in abstraction, sometimes even in hermeticism. But there is reason for mentioning Prévert and Ponge together: they are two totally opposite instances of the modern tendency to create poetry by turning it inside out.

Ponge's first important publication, *Le parti-pris des choses* (1942, Siding with Things), was probably the first application to poetry of an "objectivity" that the novel was to adopt some years later, and whose intellectual basis was phenomenology. These poems seemed at first sight very modest, limited exercises. They were like still lifes: an orange, an oyster, a fire, a snail, a shell, a pebble are described in such a way that the reader exclaims, even before he has seen the title, "Why, it's about a snail, a pebble!" Clearly, Ponge's enterprise was ambitious, and he pursued his goal with great determination.

Ponge was also careful—at the beginning at least implicitly—to give his poetry a theoretical basis. He took enormous care with these short poems, giving them the quality of models to be imitated, so as to set an example for traditional poetry. This was a challenge to the validity of poetry's claim to be an authentic, genuine contact with the world; the suspicion began to grow that poetry's territory was no more virgin than any other, that it was determined by human expectations, that its purity was sullied by human presuppositions.

Is it then nature devoid of man's presence that Ponge is seeking to evoke? Alain Robbe-Grillet recently complained that he did not admire Ponge when Ponge retained traces of anthropomorphism in his poetry. But Ponge replied that in his view any attempt to eliminate every such trace is doomed to failure. Although Ponge intended to speak not of man but of things, it is on behalf of man that he has spoken, to man, and with man's words. It is also on behalf of man: for the poems of *Siding with Things* and of his next collection, *L'œillet. La guêpe. Le mimosa* (1946, Carnation. Wasp. Mimosa), were not only exercises but, in the fullest sense, lessons drawn from things. If we have to exercise so much care in the description of a pebble, this is because the pebble is a model: it indicates to us the direction of our lives. The world of objects suppresses useless feelings and vain disquiet. Not only lyric subjectivity but also philosophical and historical problems vanish before the solidity and serenity of the object. Francis Ponge's humanism is an acceptance of the world located and defined by the object.

Curiously enough, for years Ponge was a member of the Communist Party although he did break with the party after the Liberation. However, nothing of his political commitment has ever passed into his art. He himself, as he once said, used to write as if "on the day after the revolution," anticipating the moment when we should have solved our social problems and should at last be available for the really essential thing—the object.

Humanism in the object? Yes. For if the tree or the stone has a lesson to teach us, it is that they live by their own definitions, that they are their own definitions. It is similarly our duty to live by what constitutes man, that is, by "speech and morality"—or, rather, *the morality of speech*. It is our duty to live wisely, in conformity to what is ours, following step by step, word by word, the only real things—objects.

This human labor of language became both the form

and the content of Ponge's work. His early work took up the "challenge of things to language" and sought to present a poetry that weighed the object exactly, was an equivalent for it, and had its completeness. In *Carnet du bois de pins* (1947, Pine Wood Notebook) Ponge published for the first time a succession of rough drafts, a text in its successive states. This technique recurred in *La crevette dans tous ses états* (1948, The Shrimp in All Its Stages). *La rage de l'expression* (1952, The Frenzy to Express) indicated by its title Ponge's new intention, which superseded that of "siding with things." He wanted to find in each moment of language what he was looking for: the poet's work, his gesture toward the object.

Taken to its extreme, this approach cannot produce a poem, which has to result from erasures, emendations, and recomposition: for Ponge, the poem became every word that is written down, from first to last, a verbal trajectory reproduced in its entirety, for none of its individual moments can be preferred to the progressive creation of the whole. In *La fabrique du Pré* (1971, The Field Factory), Ponge gave a succession of drafts ending with the final text of "The Field" itself. *Le savon* (1966, Soap), however, did not even contain a final text, but the progress *toward* a text, consisting of variations, passages reworked, and various stylistic exercises interspersed with reflections on the text as it was being written. In this work the impulses of the mind and the progressive emergence of the object were fused into a single effort that end with the object melting in the hands (appropriately enough, since the subject matter is soap) as the effort to describe it ends.

Is this poetry? Ponge himself has made a distinction

between what he has written and poetry, for he entitled one of his collections *Proêmes* (1949, Proems). This added "r" is the letter found in "*premier*" ("first") and "*création*" ("creation") and lacking in "*poème*." His is an anti-poetry that refuses to believe in "higher" or "complete" forms and feelings. But when the dexterity, precision, and the mobilization of all its resources enabled Ponge's poetry to capture its object, he gave language its full poetic dignity.

Henri Michaux has written against the poetic tradition, declaring that he does not care if he is a poet or not. He has used a great variety of styles, and if he has often been elliptical and incantatory, he can also be the opposite: he can write a dry, ironic, agile prose, almost like Voltaire's. All this, however, sprang from a single source, which by its nature was infinitely nearer poetry than were Ponge's objects; for Michaux, it was an inner, if also coenesthetic, experience, full of impulses and phantasms intimately linked with the body. But this "inner space," the space of poetic subjectivity, was depoeticized by Michaux's mode of expression. Thus, Michaux's approach was directly opposite to Ponge's; for as Ponge wrote, he turned what had previously been unpoetic into poetry.

Michaux's work has been unusual, and impossible to classify (it is closest to Artaud's, if one could imagine an Artaud who was in complete control of himself). He began his career long before World War II. *Mes propriétés* (My properties) was published in 1929, and *La nuit remue* (The Night in Motion) in 1935. But only since the war has the true, and considerable, worth of Michaux's poetry been recognized. His early works included diaries of actual travels (*Un barbare en Asie* [1933, A Barbarian in Asia]); logbooks of imaginary voyages in strange lands, such as *Voyage en Grande Garabagne* (1936, Voyage to Great Garabagne), in which the flora and fauna and especially the customs are described in minute detail; and *Un certain Plume* (1930, A Certain Plume), the chronicle of the life and acts of a character called Plume (Pen), who is constantly the victim of an aggressive environment. But these fables, these fictions, these utopias were used mainly to reveal and unfold the same inner world with which *My Properties* was concerned. It is a world of uneasiness and anguish, in which strong external pressures assail the protagonist, who feels out of place but who reacts, struggles, intervenes, destroying what annoys him, trying by the force of imagination, by sheer writing, to make up for what he lacks. These works were feverish but simultaneously detached and full of humor.

Michaux continued to write in this vein after World War II. *Ici, Poddéma* (1946, Here Is Poddéma) was another imaginary voyage. Poddéma is a land in which lips are put up for sale, in which words kill, in which children are manufactured to order.

But Plume broadened his experience. During the war, Michaux wrote poems in a new spirit and a new tone: anathemas, imprecations torn from him by the horror of events. In some of these he achieved a simplicity and a solemn grandeur that reminds one of the Bible (*Épreuves, Exorcismes* [1940–45, Ordeals and Exorcisms]). Michaux's obsession with death and universal emptiness joined forces with the drama of history. And thus, Michaux's work, so deliberately odd at times that it seemed delirious and even pathological, revealed a universality nonetheless.

Michaux's Plume is ultimately only a more comic version of Sartre's Roquentin and Camus's Meursault: the hero of every poem is continually wounded and disappointed, always lacks something decisive to which he cannot even give a name; he is a "pierced" man who feels only emptiness and absence inside him. Nature's infinite multiplicity weighs him down because he yearns for order and unity; but it reassures him, too, because it constitutes the mask before an emptiness that is still more terrifying. He is "between center and absence," haunted at once by obsessive absence and by excessive presence.

Michaux's work, then, is revelation and testimony. But it is something else, too—witchcraft. His purpose is "to hold at arm's length the hostile forces of the world around us." He writes for reasons of "hygiene" (as he says) and "to find a way out." Abandoning the passive Plume, Michaux has increasingly turned to this force of intervention as the motif and directing force of his works. Some of his titles bear this out: *Liberté d'action* (1945, Freedom of Action), *Poésie pour pouvoir* (1949, Poetry to Enable), *Mouvements* (1951, Movements), *Passages* (1950, 1963, Passages). The man on the run demonstrates such prodigious agility and mobility that it is impossible to grab hold of him. For Michaux, this gesture, projecting ever further, beyond the reach of all snares, defines existence and life. It is also the definition of the poem.

But in the last few years, an important development has occurred in Michaux. He has begun to identify the liberating gesture with his painting rather than with his poetry. For him, "action painting" reproduces this mobility most closely; it is mobility in action, whereas literature can never do more than describe it at a distance, after the event.

A number of collections published after 1956 have reflected Michaux's recent experiences: *Misérable miracle* (1956, Miserable Miracle), *L'infini turbulent* (1957, The Stormy Infinite), *Connaissance par les gouffres* (1961, Knowledge from the Abyss). Artificially but decisively enlarging the domain of imagination by the use of hallucinogenic drugs, Michaux began to see things he had never seen before. He used his drawings to capture his visions instantly, and the written text tended to be an analysis and commentary on events which had preceded it and which it could never entirely reproduce. In *Les grandes épreuves de l'esprit* (1966, The Great Ordeals of the Mind) he rendered still more clearly the process from re-creation to exposition, relating the unforeseen consequences of the disorientation brought about by mescaline: the derangement experienced enabled Michaux to rediscover the marvelous in ordinary experience. Ravaged consciousness can reveal what consciousness really is.

Michaux is now in a position to reply to the question, "What does getting back to normal mean?" But he has not asked us to think of normal and abnormal consciousness as opposites: it is an experience of the unity of the mind that is revealed—both in the order that normal awareness introduces into actual diversity and into emptiness—in the depersonalization of abnormal consciousness. The supreme intercession of the spirit has the power of creating a vacuum. All obstacles are flattened; all closed doors opened.

But Michaux's absolute is always shown as an activity:

it is less a vacuum than an ability to produce a vacuum, a disturbed, potential vacuum, a "peace in the midst of disruption." In his latest book, *Façons d'endormi, façons d'éveillé* (1970, Ways of a Sleeping Man, Ways of a Waking Man), he contrasted the passivity and meagerness of the night's dreams to the rich inventiveness of the "waking reverie." Thus, Michaux still seeks salvation, his always-wished-for consummation, in the same direction. But although this latest book still contained the nervous, unexpected, familiar yet dramatic diction that is inseparably Michaux's, it also showed a further development toward analysis and explanation. One can regret that Michaux has reserved the action of poetry mainly to his visual art, important though it may be.

Even if those poets just discussed reached their true stature only after the war, all had begun writing before it. What of those writing today who were not writing in 1950? What of those who were not even writing in 1960? What have they brought to poetry? And have they common features?

The contact between poetry and history, so evident in the 1940s, has continued. But those who had been only children during the Resistance recall the Nazi occupation as something not so much frightening as absurd; and they hold their elders responsible for it. Even the values that had given meaning to the struggle and to the hopes of the previous generation have now been dimmed: it is as if nothing had been worth defending or rescuing. A revolutionary atmosphere does pervade the new poetry, but the Marxist orthodoxy scarcely suits it, since Marxism is a humanism, a hope, and a heritage.

When the revolt has taken a precise political form, it

has emphasized an alienation that Marxism (a doctrine of industrially advanced countries) has tended to minimize. Édouard Glissant's (born 1928) epic poem *Les Indes* (1956, The Indies), for instance, spoke for the oppressed races and discovered behind capitalist exploitation a still more basic oppression. But the revolt of these poets has always been deeper than any political revolt could be. In the name of those young poets who felt that the world never gave them anything worthy of acceptance, Henri Pichette (born 1924), their elder by a few years, declared in his *Apoèmes* (1947, Unpoems), "I shall remake my life." And remaking one's life in this case meant remaking poetry as well.

Although Pichette, for one, adopted a precise political position in *Connaissance de la guerre* (1950, Knowledge of War), most of these writers have found the sources of their poetry outside history; whatever relationship they *do* have to history is very personal. The poet's inner anguish familiarizes him with the anguish of his epoch. And the process that brings society from alienation to unity mirrors an inner process: the moments and movements of history serve merely as landmarks and signs of private events and impulses.

This new poetry often relates to an experience realized in successive moments, but moments of *inner* time—an experience whose starting point is emptiness and absence, conjoined with or reflected in an absence of language and an inability to speak. Is expression possible? Is language possible? For the most part philosophers who have read Hegel, Sartre, and Blanchot, these younger poets know that the word is the thing's absence, that language brings death into the world. The poet takes his vows to the world through the intermediary of language, but he sees language's impotence to touch reality. Speech is empty, the world is separate: such is the starting point. But whereas their elders would be content to assert this experience, leaving themselves free to deny it at the same time, and leaving readers and critics the task of harmonizing these two opposite assertions, most of the newcomers do not so much juxtapose the data of the immediately lived experience as describe a trajectory, a thought-out itinerary. Poetry must pass from dead language to living speech that is in tune with the world. This passage from one language to another—always poetry's fundamental thrust —has often been linked with another sort of passage— that from an alienated to a liberated society.

Among poets who have come to prominence since 1950, the leading figure has been Yves Bonnefoy. His *Du mouvement et de l'immobilité de Douve* (1953, On the Motion and Immobility of Douve) precisely embodied the inner dialectic I have just been describing. Douve is poetic utterance. Dying, dead, reborn, identified with nature, grass, flint, and then with consciousness and language, motionless and immobile, maenad, salamander, woman's body, or half-effaced fresco on the walls of a chapel, Douve incarnates poetic utterance in all its ambiguity and its metamorphoses. Of this collection of poetry, one could say that poetry alone is the subject.

But poetry so understood is everything, both language and world. To begin with, poetry and life seem impossible. They are dead, dead by reason of everything which is negative in human experience and which can only be evoked by the assemblage of all the shapes of nothingness: physical dissolution, silence, absence, desert, night. To speak the "true name," the poet must appeal to all these fragmentary names, sketch all the many profiles of a single absence. And the poem, in part, celebrates an entombment; but it also (and ultimately) celebrates a resurrection. From absence to presence, from silence to speech, a motion occurs. Better still: the word must be founded on the initial silence, life must be founded upon death.

This dialectic, by which the experience of nothingness becomes the guarantee of any assertion of authentic life, gives Bonnefoy's work its sense and its life. *Vrai corps* (True Body), a poem in *On the Motion and Immobility of Douve*, evokes the corpse made everlasting by the word denoting it. Night is "other than night"; night is a "buried day" that can be delivered from the tomb; one needs only to assert it and pass through it. The collection's epigraph is a statement by Hegel which Georges Bataille also loved to quote and which illuminates the broadest landscape of contemporary thought and feeling: "The life of the mind is not afraid of death and does not try to steer clear of it. It is a life that copes with death and sustains itself within it."

Bonnefoy's subsequent collections of poetry, *Hier régnant désert* (1958, Yesterday Reigning Desert) and *Pierre écrite* (1963, Written Stone)—as well as *L'improbable* (1959, The Improbable) and *Un rêve fait à Mantoue* (1957, A Mantuan Dream), essays largely about painting, in which we find again the "erudite music" of the poet—showed Bonnefoy pursuing the same ideas, but in a less abstract and more polished way. *Yesterday Reigning Desert* and *Written Stone* were not assemblages of poems, but single books, works that have their own rules of sequence and are conceived of as wholes. Hand in hand with this mastery of form went a certain metrical traditionalism that sometimes included rhyme and the alexandrine line.

Bonnefoy's recent collections have blended the impulses of life and of literary creation more closely together. His writing still shows occasional moments of the harmony noticeable in his early collections. But he now refuses to accept such relief, such a refuge: the confident lyrical excitement of Bonnefoy's powerful verse is punctuated by short, terse, dismembered texts—"written stones," like to many epitaphs inscribed on tombstones. "Modern poetry is a long way from its possible home. It is still banished from the great hall with the four windows. The repose of form in the poem cannot be honestly accepted," wrote Bonnefoy; and he is more and more convinced of it. On the other hand, although the spiritual horizon is by no means lost sight of, the actual details of his progress concern the poet more deeply: in a poem like *La chambre* (The Room) the awareness of unity occurs in the here and now, is embodied in a simple human love.

André du Bouchet (born 1924) and Jacques Dupin (born 1927) have much in common with Yves Bonnefoy, with whom they share the editorship of the review *L'éphémère*. They resemble him in their language, too, which both seeks and rejects its form, and accepts a special poetic order of experience. But unlike Bonnefoy, they employ styles that are dense, sometimes aphoristic. And the blank spaces on the page play a considerable part, especially with Bouchet.

Bouchet, in *Dans la chaleur vacante* (1961, In the

Vacant Heat) and *Où le soleil* (1969, Where the Sun) attempted to capture in the crystallization of brief poems the glare of a moment of dazzlement and vertigo. His dense, aphoristic style, and a typographical arrangement that sometimes suggests the poem as object, evoke the fullness of experience without pretending to an impossible formal perfection. It is a poetry of blinding fissures, and the text is split and torn by blanks and silences a little like Reverdy's poetry.

Jacques Dupin, in a work like *Gravir* (1963, To Climb), has also preserved the jagged abruptness of an experience against which language shatters. But the melody of the prose poem (not unlike Char's) often introduces moments of relief, almost of seduction. With less force and more simplicity, Jean-Claude Renard (born 1922) has been concerned with the same kind of experience, but with religious overtones, as can be seen in *La terre du sacre* (1966, The Land of the Rite).

Among younger poets who have revealed a lyrical voice, the most moving has been Jacques Réda (born 1929), who in a work like *Récitatif* (1970, Recitative) sometimes recalls the muted harmonies of Rilke. Michel Deguy's (born 1930) poetry, such as *Biefs* (1963, Watercourses) and *Actes* (1966, Acts), has been much more intellectual and cryptic. Deguy has moved close to pure experimentation with the written word, rejecting all reference to poetic experience.

Other young poets (those associated for instance with the review *Tel Quel*) are principally interested in the permutations of a language that, they claim, has nothing to say. The poem speaks of nothing, of nobody. It is anonymous and incessant language, and has no other meaning than its literal text, its "textuality." Marcelin

Pleynet (born 1933) and Denis Roche have written poems that would be reminiscent of the "automatic writing" of surrealism if it were not for surrealism's special intensity that compels us to call it poetry. However, the texts of *Tel Quel* writers are easily interchangeable with prose. Lines often end with a hyphen cutting the word in two, just as in prose. More importantly, the "electricity" of poetry is totally absent. However, Pleynet and Roche still use such differentiating descriptive titles as "poems" or "stories." And in their "poetry" they have utilized blank spaces and divisions into lines, as in formal poetry. Even when meanings and genres are destroyed, something still remains to prevent literature from becoming nothing more than the unified field of a meaningless "textuality."

Jacques Roubaud (born 1932)—whose texts, too, may seem to be in some limbo between prose and poetry—has concerns of a structuralist nature, concerns similarly reflected in the most recent texts of Robbe-Grillet and Michel Butor. In ϵ (1969, ϵ [epsilon]) Roubaud neither surrendered to automatic writing nor sought to compose the absolute book, but organized the work in such a way that it can support various interpretations and various arrangements. Four different readings are suggested for ϵ: one according to the way the texts are arranged, a second according to a system of mathematical signs, a third following the progress of a game of Japanese *go*, and a fourth by reading each text separately. But these permutations are ultimately less interesting than what each reader can do with the work; and one has to admit that Roubaud is highly inventive and that he even possesses the electricity that disappeared after the demise of surrealism.

7

THE THEATER:
BETWEEN LITERATURE
AND SPECTACLE

Some of the most important dramatists of the contemporary period have also been novelists—and, more generally, simply *writers*. These include Henry de Montherlant, Jean-Paul Sartre, Albert Camus, Jean Genet, and Samuel Beckett, all of whose total literary activity I have already discussed. Perhaps—particularly abroad—they are better known as writers for the stage. But I felt it wiser to discuss their literary work as a whole together with related writers who are primarily or exclusively novelists.

Whether their plays have been produced or not, whether they have been successful or not on the stage, almost all of them can be read as independent text. Whether or not they retain a place in theater repertories, they will always merit attention on the shelves of libraries.

Significantly, none of these five writers began his career with the drama: each of them was temperamentally a novelist, and the theater, far from being an exclusive and spontaneous vocation, was merely one form that their literary calling took for a time. The hero who underwent successive incarnations in Montherlant's plays originated in the 1935 essay *Service inutile* (Useless Service), which defined this character and his dilemma of being caught between a desire for commitment and a nihilistic clarity of mind. Sartre used the drama to simplify his metaphysics and his ethics, to give them a wider audience and a greater influence. Camus, it is true, was always interested in the theater for its own sake, but his fiction was certainly more artistically successful.

Genet's plays, on the other hand, are both the best known and the most convincing part of his work; but much of their strength derives from his poetic and narrative gifts. And although the audience for Beckett's plays is certainly larger than the readership of his novels, he was first and above all a novelist. In this section, I shall therefore focus on those authors who have written exclusively for the theater—or those at least for whom the drama is their prime mode of expression—and on those sociological considerations peculiar to the theater. However, since the development of the contemporary drama has followed a pattern similar to that of the novel, a number of general points have already been established.

Through the years, there have been some novelists, like Jules Romains, whose dramatic work has crowned their careers. Others, like Balzac and Stendhal, Gide and Martin du Gard, met with great failure in the theater. A number of contemporary novelists have written some first-rate plays. But they remain marginal to their fiction. After the success of *Asmodée* (1937, Asmodée), Fran-

çois Mauriac wrote *Les mal aimés* (1945, The Ill-Beloved)
and *Le feu sur la terre* (1951, Fire on the Earth); but he
will be remembered chiefly for his novels. The same can
be said of Julien Green, although *Sud* (1953, South), the
drama of an impossible and guilty homosexual love affair
set during the American civil war, and *L'ennemi* (1954,
The Enemy), which treated similar themes transposed to
prerevolutionary France, were both fine plays. Since his
first play, *The Fisher King*, in 1948, Julien Gracq has
written nothing for the stage. And Georges Bernanos's
admirable play *Dialogues of the Carmelites*, published
posthumously in 1949, and not produced until 1952, owed
its existence to an accident resulting from a commission:
Bernanos had been asked to write a screen adaptation of
Gertrud von Le Fort's novella *Die Letzte am Schafott*.

A number of novelistic masterpieces have been successfully adopted for the stage, most notably Faulkner's
Requiem for a Nun by Camus as *Requiem pour une
nonne* (1957) and Kafka's *Der Prozeß* by Gide and
Jean-Louis Barrault as *Le procès* (1947, The Trial). Indeed, their version of *The Trial* foreshadowed some of
the later features of the *"nouveau théâtre."*

For there is a new theater just as there is a new novel.
Paris greeted Giraudoux's *La folle de Chaillot* (1945, The
Madwoman of Chaillot) right after the war with an
acclaim that suggested that everything was going to continue as it had before the war. Here was Giraudoux working again with Louis Jouvet—a collaboration that had
dominated the prewar theater. (Here, too, was the established stage designer Christian Bérard and the actress
Marguerite Moreno, a great name since the beginning of
the century.) Continuity of tradition was not to be, how-

ever. Ironically, Jouvet, who produced Giraudoux's last great success, in 1951 was to produce Genet's *The Maids*, one of the earliest masterpieces of the new theater.

The gulf between old and new was as marked in the theater as in other genres. And even before the appearance of completely new departures in the theater, a change in theatrical style seemed to be in the air. Although Paul Claudel's plays were all written before 1940, most were not produced until 1943, the date of Jean-Louis Barrault's production of *Le soulier de satin* (1929, The Satin Slipper). After the war Claudel's work found an increasingly important place in the repertory. This was not only true in Paris, where Barrault produced *Partage de midi* (1906, Break of Noon), *L'échange* (1901, The Exchange), *Le livre de Christophe Colomb* (1930, The Book of Christopher Columbus), and *Tête d'or* (1891, Golden Head), and where the T.N.P. (Théâtre National Populaire) produced *La ville* (1893, The City) and Jean-Marie Serreau *L'otage* (1911, The Hostage). Claudel was also produced in the provinces by a whole flock of young companies who had established themselves. In addition to Claudel, the most important playwrights represented in the repertories of the new theaters were Brecht and García Lorca. As a result, the stage was invaded by a lyricism and by the search for a modern epic mode, prompting a new awareness of our period by replacing cliché-ridden naturalism with a new distance between stage and spectator.

The theatergoing public has greatly increased, although there is still a potential audience that young producers have not yet reached, an audience they feel has been confined to ghettos by capitalist society. Nonetheless, plays are now produced even for small audiences and brief runs. The theater's variety and daring can thus rival that of the printed book (for a play production's financial outlay is now not much larger than a book's). Little experimental theaters have sprung up everywhere (Théâtre des Noctambules. Théâtre de Poche, Théâtre de la Huchette, Théâtre du Quartier Latin, Théâtre de Babylone, Théâtre de Lutèce); they manage to survive on tiny budgets provided by private donations. In the provinces, subsidized dramatic centers created by the French government have some freedom from commercial pressures, and apparently no political strings are attached. In addition, festivals, supported mainly by local councils, have proliferated. All these new conditions explain fresh departures in both stage production and repertory, and they also explain the increased freedom with the audience and with theatrical convention.

Nonetheless, there is still a traditional theater, just as there is still a traditional novel, and the former is perhaps even more alive than the latter, for audiences keep to their old habits even more fondly than do readers. The easy theater, the *théâtre du boulevard*, gives the public exactly what it expects: its function is to amuse; and its habit is to produce suspense in the audience, as Thierry Maulnier (born 1909, pseudonym of Jacques Talagrand) said in his preface to *Le profanateur* (1952, The Desecrator), "over some gentleman's chances of sleeping with some lady in the last act, or over some lady's chances of rearousing the passions of some gentleman." The "masterpieces" of this sort of theater sometimes run for years, but they are then replaced by other successes that assume exactly the same function and so consign the earlier "masterpieces" to oblivion. Since they do not survive by virtue of their texts, they do not belong to literature—whose nature it is to leave a history behind it.

But there is an intermediary ground between such rapidly forgotten successes and works that play a lasting part in literary history. Some certainly very "slick" plays are not without quality. Among these are André Roussin's (born 1911) *Am Stram Gram* (1944, Am Stram Gram) and *La petite hutte* (1947, The Little Hut), Roger Ferdinand's (born 1898) *Les croulants se portent bien* (1959, Rip Van Winkle's Doing Well), the enormous output of Pierre Barillet (born 1923) and Jean-Pierre Grédy (born 1920), or the amusing spectacles of Robert Dhéry (born 1921). Such is the domain of the *théâtre du boulevard*.

There is also a theater whose traditional nature guarantees it an audience but which certainly also belongs to literature; one thinks of Sacha Guitry (1885–1957), Jean Sarment (born 1897), Stève Passeur (born 1899), Paul Raynal (born 1885), and Édouard Bourdet (1887–1945). But the works of these men belong mainly to the prewar period, as does Marcel Pagnol's (born 1895) famous trilogy—*Marius* (1929, Marius), *Fanny* (1931, Fanny), and *César* (1937, César)—which has kept a place in theater repertories.

After the war, the spirit of the traditional theater underwent a radical change. To embody an awareness of the altered world situation, it felt obliged to change its content—though not its form. "Our epoch is an historical and metaphysical one," wrote Maulnier in the previously mentioned preface. "A sheltered bourgeoisie used to live at ease with its dreams, between four comfortable walls. These walls have collapsed in the storm and have let in the cold and the darkness, the problems of crime and human unhappiness, the dumb questionings of creation in its death throes."

The majority of plays dating from during or just after the war were concerned with the problems of the contemporary world. But a poetic mythology—as in Jean Cocteau's *Renaud et Armide* (1943, Renaud and Armide) and Maurice Clavel's (born 1920) *Les incendiaires* (1946, The Incendiaries)—or an historical framework often achieved the effect of distance. Ancient mythology and history had been drawn upon by Giraudoux, and were used again by Jean Anouilh (born 1910) in *Antigone* (1943, Antigone), by Sartre in *The Flies*, by Georges Neveux (born 1900) in *Le voyage de Thésée* (1943, The Voyage of Theseus), by Emmanuel Roblès (born 1914) in *Montserrat* (1948, Montserrat), by Thierry Maulnier in *The Desecrator*, and by Gabriel Marcel (born 1889) in *Rome n'est plus dans Rome* (1951, Rome Is No Longer in Rome).

Whether they used an historical framework or not, there were many works that can be defined as "problem plays," whose themes were taken from contemporary events—among them Georges Neveux's *La voleuse de Londres* (1960, The Lady Thief from London), Emmanuel Roblès's *La vérité est morte* (1952, Truth Is Dead), Claude-André Puget's (born 1905) *La peine capitale* (1948, Capital Punishment), and André Obey's (born 1892) *Maria* (1946, Maria) and *Les trois coups de minuit* (1958, The Curtain Rises at Midnight).

These "problem plays" had the inherent dangers of didacticism and artifice. A comic treatment of similar

themes had better chances of avoiding these dangers.
There has been much verve and inventiveness in Félicien
Marceau's (born 1913) plays; the technical originality of
L'œuf (1956, The Egg) and *La bonne soupe* (1958, The
Good Soup) consisted in their being almost entirely
monologues. Marceau's *Babour* (1959, Babour) amus-
ingly probed the problems of sex in contemporary society. Equally lively has been Marcel Aymé's drama:
Lucienne et le boucher (1947, Lucienne and the Butcher);
Clérambard (1950, Clérambard); *Les oiseaux de lune*
(1955, The Moon Birds), in which a strange individual
has the power to turn his acquaintances into birds; and
La convention Belzébir (1966, The Belzébir Convention), which takes place in a society that permits murder
upon payment of a fee. The price both Marceau and
Aymé paid for their ability to entertain was a certain
vulgarity. But neither was as vulgar as Marcel Achard
(born 1899), who added a few further commercial successes to his copious prewar output: *Auprès de ma
blonde* (1946, Beside My Blonde), *Savez-vous planter
les choux* (1951, Can You Plant Cabbages?), and especially *Patate* (1957, Spud).

In a very different category are Armand Salacrou (born
1899) and Jean Anouilh, both of whom have written
exclusively for the stage. They are the two playwrights
who can be compared most closely to the novelists of
the same period. Their work has contained an equivalent
for what I have already described in the existentialist
novel. They combined a new content—in the sense that
evident contemporaneity is mingled with a pessimistic
and accusatory vision—with an evolution in form, which,
however, never threatened to push content into the background.

Salacrou in *L'inconnue d'Arras* (1935, The Unknown Woman from Arras) was toying with a metaphysical theater. This was a play that, "like our lives, emerges from nothingness only to return to it." But his plays between 1946 and 1961 were primarily concerned with social criticisms: *Les nuits de la colère* (1946, Nights of Wrath), whose subject was the Resistance; *L'archipel Lenoir* (1947, Lenoir Archipelago); *Une femme trop honnête* (1955, Too Virtuous a Woman), which satirized the bourgeois family; and *Boulevard Durand* (1960, Boulevard Durand), in which justice miscarries because of political allegiances.

A mainspring of Jean Anouilh's work has been a savage indictment of society, despite his belonging to the political right (although there is, to be sure, the phenomenon of right-wing anarchism). His work has had an abundance and diversity that puts it in the first rank. Anouilh was famous before the war for *L'hermine* (1931, The Ermine), *Le voyageur sans bagage* (1936, Traveler without Luggage), and *La sauvage* (1934, The Savage). In these, the Anouilh hero, obsessed by youthful idealism and rejecting the compromises of ordinary life, appeared in various guises. *Antigone* gave the Anouilh hero (or heroine, in this case) the prestige of an ancient myth. Creon, who accepts the demands society makes on the individual, is not an entirely contemptible figure, but the play is naturally dominated by Antigone herself, whose unreasonable behavior is seen as reasonable.

This conflict (close to the one we find in Montherlant) between personal purity and the demands of society tended, after the war, to disappear in Anouilh's work in favor of a savage pessimism that rejected any alternative. His early division of his plays into the *pièces noires* and the *pièces roses* gave way to a uniform atmosphere of sourness and asperity. *Ardèle, ou la marguerite* (1948, Ardèle, or the Daisy) was a pitiless debunking of all respectability and all enthusiasm. A sexuality of resentment, not unlike that found in Sartre's novels, was expressed in the harrowing scene in which two children parody their parents' dissolute behavior. In *La valse des toréadors* (1952, The Waltz of the Toreadors) and *Le boulanger, la boulangère et le petit mitron* (1968, The Baker, the Baker's Wife, and the Little Baker's Boy) Anouilh continued this picture of incurable degradation and disgust. This exaggerated pessimism seems to have been caused largely by the events of the Liberation of France, which Anouilh felt had involved excess and injustice, proving that evil inevitably results from the illusion of good.

Anouilh's attitude toward current events perhaps explains the temporal distancing he sought through his historical plays. (Did the break with the present drive Anouilh, like Giono, back toward the past? Or did the past serve Anouilh merely as a prudent disguise?) *Becket, ou l'honneur de Dieu* (1959, Becket, or the Honor of God) reasserted the absurdity of the noblest conflicts, and *La foire d'empoigne* (1960, Catch as Catch Can) put Louis XVIII in a better light than Napoleon. In *L'alouette* (1953, The Lark) the trial of Joan of Arc offered many analogies to the contemporary world. And in *Pauvre Bitos* (1958, Poor Bitos) a magistrate who has terrorized his town just after the Liberation is persuaded to adopt the role of Robespierre at a fancy dress party.

In his most recent plays—*Cher Antoine* (1969, Dear Antoine) and *Les poissons rouges* (1970, The Goldfish)—Anouilh adopted a more confidential, autobiographical form; but he obsessively continued to attack social hypocrisy, above all the vacillations of progress and progressivist optimism. Anouilh has experimented ingeniously, sometimes daringly, in almost all of his plays: plays within plays, liberties taken with time, and so forth. But he has remained traditional in that he links a quite explicit content, based usually upon a central problem, to a form that primarily seeks to effect a convincing illusion of reality. Anouilh is neither a Beckett nor a Eugène Ionesco (born 1909), but he was one of the first to pay tribute to Beckett's *Waiting for Godot* and to Ionesco's *Les chaises* (1952, The Chairs).

Nonetheless, it was the kind of drama practiced by Anouilh that Ionesco denounced in 1953: "Our contemporary theater . . . does not fit the cultural style of our epoch; it is out of tune with the spirit of our times." This is because only its content had changed: it had shown us men of a different society and a different psychology. But we should go further, and ask if man exists at all as a being who can be expressed immediately and straightforwardly. We should go as far as putting everything in parentheses, using language and the stage setting like rockets and explosives—lighting up one knows not what. Neither Sartre nor Camus brought any real transformation about in the theater, any more than they did in the novel. And, of course, the trouble was that they were novelists. Is it not *poetry* that brings about the most radical changes?

Giraudoux's drama, today so unjustly neglected, had been a prewar expression of the tendency to transform the theater. But the true precursors of the new theater are to be found in surrealism and its forerunners. This tradition runs from Alfred Jarry's (1873–1907) *Ubu roi* (1897, King Ubu) to Apollinaire's *Les mamelles de Tirésias* (1918, The Breasts of Tiresias), from Tristan Tzara's *La première aventure céleste de M. Antipyrine* (1916, The First Celestial Adventure of Mr. Antipyrine) to Antonin Artaud's *The Cenci* to Roger Vitrac's (1899–1952) *Victor, ou les enfants au pouvoir* (Victor, or Children in Power), which dates from 1928, but only achieved a really appreciative audience when it was revived in 1962. Slowly, these plays established a countertradition leading the theater to reject realism and the portrayal of society, and laying it open to fantasy, dream, and word play.

Most of Michel de Ghelderode's (1898–1962) plays were written before 1940. Only after 1945, however, did new conditions in the theater allow him to achieve decisive successes on the stage with *Hop, Signor!* (1942, Hop, Signor!) and *Fastes d'enfer* (1938, Chronicles of Hell). These masterpieces linked burlesque, diablerie, and—despite Ghelderode's refusal to consider himself a philosopher—a metaphysical vision of the world to a lively verbal talent.

Boris Vian, too, may be classified with the precursors of the new theater. *Les bâtisseurs d'empire* (The Empire Builders), it is true, was written in 1959, and seemed to look like the work of a disciple, for Ionesco's influence was so visible in it. But *L'équarissage pour tous* (1947, Knackering for All) anticipated many future developments in the drama.

To a still-traditional form of poetic theater belonged the plays of Jules Supervielle, whose *The Child Stealer* was produced in 1948, and whose *Shéhérazade* (1949,

Scheherazade) was put on that same year at the Festival of Avignon by Jean Vilar. The poetry that flows through Georges Schehadé's plays is more unusual and, one might say, more modern. In *Mr. Bob'le, La soirée des proverbes* (1954, Evening of Proverbs), *L'histoire de Vasco* (1956, The Tale of Vasco), and *L'émigré de Brisbane* (1965, The Brisbane Émigré), he embodied a fresh and charming lyricism in a group of familar and preposterous characters who meet as memory or quest dictate.

Aimé Césaire's *La tragédie du roi Christophe* (1964, The Tragedy of King Christophe) was a poet's play but also a political play calculated to serve "black power." It depicted a native king of Haiti at the beginning of the nineteenth century, who embodies the independence of his people but who is abandoned by them. *Une saison au Congo* (1966, A Season in the Congo) recounted the events that led to the death of Patrice Lumumba. Césaire's theater has occupied a place halfway between Claudel's and Brecht's.

The springs of a violent lyricism based on Arthur Rimbaud (1854–1891) and on surrealism meet, in Henri Pichette's plays, in the accents of accusation and commitment. But *Les épiphanies* (1947, the Epiphanies) and *Nucléa* (1952, Nucléa), a play against war and atomic destruction, were more like oratorios than plays, poems entrusted to an actor's voice. Their success was largely due to the presence of Gérard Philippe on the stage.

Jacques Audiberti, on the other hand, although a novelist and poet was a true man of the theater in his plays. *Quoat quoat* (1946, Quoat Quoat), *Evil Is in the Air*, *L'effet Glapion* (1959, The Glapion Effect) were firmly based on the structures of the drama. Their verve, fantasy, and baroque effervescence are cleverly linked to a symbolic action, whose development carries us vigorously along. *Evil Is in the Air* was Audiberti's masterpiece, and no doubt one of the best plays produced since World War II. Its freedom and its clowning did not hide its profundity. Although Audiberti had no explicit philosophy, he told us himself that he "never deviated from this single subject, the conflict between good and evil, between soul and flesh . . . incarnation."

The most recent theater has been characterized by two tendencies: a manipulation of language that revolutionized theatrical form and led to a questioning of language itself; and an exploration of psychology and of society. Some plays have clearly been on one side or other of this division; some have deliberately been on the border. Jean Tardieu has mastered the minor theatrical form of "stylistic exercises"—not full-length plays but playlets, monologues, and humorous sketches for small-scale theaters or cabarets. *Il y avait foule au manoir* (1955, The Crowd Up at the Manor) and *Ce que parler veut dire* (1955, What Talking Means). The contemporaneity of Tardieu's plays comes from their giving the problem of language its due; he is far indeed from any sociological interest.

René de Obaldia (born 1918) has written novels, notably *Tamerlan des cœurs* (1955, Tamburlaine of Hearts), as well as a number of richly parodic plays, in which one finds that rare combination of amusement and intelligence. His "chamber western," *Du vent dans les branches de sassafras* (1965, Wind in the Branches of the Sassafras), has been his best play to date. There was also burlesque and the inventiveness of the highest comedy in Roland Dubillard's (born 1923) *Naïves hirondelles* (1961,

Naïve Swallows), *La maison d'os* (1962, The House of Bone), and *Le jardin de betteraves* (1969, The Sugar-Beet Garden)—but also much anguish and disquiet. The "house of bone" is the body about to give up its consciousness in a long death agony.

The theater of Jean Vauthier (born 1910) has been a theater of language. He, too, has been concerned with the condition of man rather than of society. *Capitaine Bada* (1952, Captain Bada), his best work to date, was an extraordinary monologue that exteriorized the dreams and fantasies of the hero, a would-be author who is prevented from writing by words.

The political theater is, however, at least in quantitative terms, even more important than the poetic theater, and Brecht has had an enormous influence over the past several decades. No longer addressing themselves to the traditional middle-class public but to the working class, these playwrights and directors have sought to make contact through their new public's preoccupations, which are societal and revolutionary. The majority of the regional dramatic centers and young companies have a distinctly political outlook. A good example is the Théâtre National Populaire, directed by Jean Vilar from 1951, the year of its foundation, until 1963. His successor, Georges Wilson, who has recently left, somewhat reduced these political tendencies.

The development of Arthur Adamov's (1908–1970) career was representative of the movement from the inner to the outer, from the poetic to the political. Although his first plays, including *Le professeur Taranne* (1953, Professor Taranne), attacked, in the tradition of Strindberg and Ionesco, the human image itself, in *Le ping-*

pong (1955, Ping Pong) the slot machine, which is the
play's central character, is primarily a symbol of the
regimented society Adamov was rebelling against. In
Paolo Paoli (1957, Paolo Paoli), *La politique des restes*
(1967, The Politics of the Remainder) and *Off Limits*
(1969, the title is in English) he deepened this political
commitment and showed a tendency to return to realism.
Adamov's schizophrenic lyricism reached its limit and
found its antidote, as the author himself put it, in the
awareness that the object (the slot machine for instance)
was the "product of a particular society" and has a "particular purpose: to earn money and prestige."

Georges Michel's (born 1926) plays—*La promenade
du dimanche* (1967, The Sunday Walk), *L'agression*
(1967, Aggression)—belong to the theater of social criticism, as do Armand Gatti's (born 1924) *La vie imaginaire de l'éboueur Auguste Geai* (1962, The Imaginary
Life of Auguste Geai the Street Cleaner), *Chant public
devant deux chaises électriques* (1964, Public Song before
Two Electric Chairs), and *V comme Vietnam* (1967, V
for Vietnam). Gatti has shown the tendency to get lost
in a maze of divergent experiments with technique. The
plays of François Billetdoux (born 1927)—*Tchin-tchin*
(1959, Tchin-Tchin), *Va donc chez Törpe* (1961, Well,
Go Along to Törpe's Place), *Comment va le monde,
mössieu? Il tourne, mössieu!* (1964, How Is the World
Mister? It's Turning, Mister!)—have been clever, perhaps too clever. Billetdoux has followed the same socially
critical path as has Gatti, but Billetdoux knows how to
achieve distance and the trappings of myth.

More complex, and finding a unity among the various
movements in a theater that reflects the personality of

a writer (novelist or poet), have been the plays of Robert Pinget (*Lettre morte* [1959, Dead Letter]); Marguerite Duras (*Le square* [1957, The Square], *L'amante anglaise* [1968, The English Mistress]); Nathalie Sarraute (*Le silence* [1964, Silence], *Le mensonge* [1966, The Lie]); and Romain Weingarten (born 1926) (*Akara* [1948, Akara], *L'été* [1966, Summer]). But it is clearly in the plays of Samuel Beckett and Jean Genet that theater expressing the personality of the writer has achieved its highest expression.

Eugène Ionesco, who came to France from Rumania in 1945, is the only writer of recent years who has earned an important place in literary history through his plays alone. His other writings, such as *Journal en miettes* (1967, Fragments of a Journal), have not been creations of a different kind, but commentaries on his one mode of creation. Rather like Samuel Beckett, Ionesco also had to face the possibility of capitulating before his philosophical dilemmas and his struggle with language. Instead, both dramatists have created work that is in a sense classic, ample, and constantly developing, nourished by spontaneous inspiration, and sustained by the supreme mastery of the structures of expression.

Like Adamov and others, Ionesco has passed from an anti-theater limited to quirks of language and reflections of the inner self to a discussion of the problems of contemporary society. But Ionesco has been almost the only one to link a revolution in literary form to a rejection of political revolution, for his pessimism about history is the inevitable outgrowth of the pessimism of his philosophy.

Ionesco's first plays, all one-acters, which so questioned

language and the theater itself, found an audience in the tiny experimental theaters, such as the Théâtre des Noctambules and the Théâtre de la Huchette. If we are to take Ionesco's word for it, his first effort at playwriting was an unexpected consequence of his starting to learn English by the audio-visual method. Nothing could have been further from his mind than an interest in the theater; but he suddenly saw that the elements of cliché, the unexpected, the discontinuity, and the pointlessness of the conversation examples contained in the lessons were infinitely more comic power than all the plays in the repertory.

His first intention was thus to push to the extreme those elements of rupture, absurdity, and artifice inherent in language and drama, and to obtain from this exaggeration new forms of comedy and tragedy, something that at any rate would be extreme and intolerable. In *La leçon* (1950, The Lesson) and *La cantatrice chauve* (1948, The Bald Soprano) the characters were little more than the mouthpieces for disjointed speech: their marionette- or robot-like gestures indicated how language can turn us into machines. At the same time, the gestures parodied the traditional theater. Here, as Ionesco said in *Jacques, ou la soumission* (1950, Jack, or the Submission), "the drawing-room comedy decomposes and goes mad!" In *The Chairs* Ionesco took his investigation further. Two old people get a deaf-mute orator to transmit an incomprehensible message, after their suicides, to an audience of empty chairs. This message no longer represents the emptiness only of language but of life and of the universe.

As Ionesco's drama has developed, it has expanded.

Amédée, ou comment s'en débarrasser (1954, Amédée, or How to Get Rid of It) was his first three-act play. A single room no longer limits the action; there is also a street, a town and its inhabitants, the sky and its stars. There is an action, which passes through a series of comic modes (and through the parody of tragedy) to an incredible conclusion. The language has an appropriateness to what is talked about, even if that something is nothing; it is dry, terse, restrained.

But it was not really until Ionesco's next plays, in which the character of Béranger appears—*Tueur sans gages* (1957, Killer without Wages), *Le rhinocéros* (1959, Rhinoceros), *Le piéton de l'air* (1962, A Stroll in the Air), *Le roi se meurt* (1962, The King Is Dying)—that he began to relate his questions (which remained, of course, primarily metaphysical) to the contemporary period and its problems. "It is not a particular society that I feel to be absurd; it is man himself," he has said clearly. One can see, however, how society piles absurdity upon this absurdity: in *Rhinoceros* all the characters turn into insensitive pachyderms, in front of the "hero," who remains isolated in his humanity; and this is how a country becomes nazified or bolshevized.

In *A Stroll in the Air* Ionesco looked at an unreal world, which he called an anti-world: the hero rises at first into the air, as if thanks to a mystical experience, and gazes about him as if he were seeing for the first time; however, eventually he falls back onto an earth covered with mire and blood. There is no escape. In *The King Is Dying* Ionesco presented a striking image of human life as a progress toward death: Béranger I, a derisory king, accompanied by a servant, a guard, his two wives, and a doctor-executioner, performs the stages of a ceremony that ends in nothingness. In *La soif et la faim* (1964, Thirst and Hunger) Ionesco took up similar themes less convincingly.

Ionesco has offered no solutions, unless it be in the catharsis of the theater, its laughter or its derision (despite Ionesco's declaration that he only resorts to humor out of habit). Amid disquiet and risibility, amid shock elements that are sometimes comic and sometimes disturbing, we are presented with the paradox of creation following its course, although the course leads nowhere.

The new theater of Ionesco, Genet, Beckett, and Adamov is beginning to look traditional. For they have not really altered the relationship between play and spectator. Brecht had attempted to alter that relationship through distancing alienation—an approach that insisted that the theater is not life. The newest trend in altering the function of the theater has been a reversal of Brecht's approach. Continuing Artaud's protest and demands, under the immediate influence of the American troupe The Living Theatre and of the Polish director Jerzy Grotowski, whose *The Constant Prince* was a great success in Paris in 1968, the youngest playwrights and directors (frequently one man occupies both functions) have sought a mixture of theater and life that will abolish the footlights, the separation between stage and spectators. They have also sought to eliminate the text as a previously written and complete creation, in favor of a collective improvization, a "happening."

In this participatory theater, there is a nostalgia for a primitive state of affairs when the theater was a collective celebration, a longing for total liberation, or rather the annihilation of the individual in favor of a communal ecstasy. It is a Dionysian theater, in which bodily expression matters more than the text.

Fernando Arrabal (born 1932), who has written, among other plays, *Le cimetière des voitures* (1958, The Automobile Graveyard), defined the theater in terms that were clearly reminiscent of Artaud:

> At present, a number of different personalities in different parts of the world are trying to create a form of theater pushed to its ultimate consequences. Despite the enormous differences between our efforts, we are turning theater into a festival, a ceremony built on a rigorous pattern. Tragedy and puppet show, poetry and vulgarity, comedy and melodrama, love and eroticism, happening and set theory, bad taste and aesthetic refinement, sacrilege and the sacred, condemnation to death and exaltation of life, the sordid and the sublime, are natural parts of this festival, this ceremony of Pan.

Whatever the future of such experiments may be, they cannot by definition form part of literature. Drama has in the past been simultaneously text and spectacle; this is why it has never completely belonged to the history of literature. But if it becomes no more than a spectacle, a demonstration, a moment in the life of the collectivity, it will cease to have anything at all to do with literature.

8

FROM CREATION
TO CRITICISM

Can the essay be considered a creative genre? It would
be overly hasty to answer no, for at certain periods, the
greatest works of French literature have been essays—
first and foremost the writings of Michel Montaigne
(1553–1592). But although Blaise Pascal (1623–1662),
Charles-Louise de Montesquieu (1689–1755), and Montaigne himself never wrote poetry or fiction, it has only
rarely happened in French literature that a great author
wrote nothing but essays. Jean-Jacques Rousseau (1712–
1782) wrote the novel *Julie ou la nouvelle Héloise* (1761,
Julie, or The New Eloise), Voltaire wrote *Candide*
(1759, Candide), not to mention his dramatic works.

The role of the essay has been important since World
War II. Sartre and Camus were major essayists as well
as novelists and playwrights. Georges Bataille's literary
contribution is difficult to classify; but if a genre must
be applied, it most closely resembles the essay. Jean
Paulhan—in works from *The Flowers of Tarbes* and *Clef
de la poesie* (1944, The Key to Poetry) to *La preuve par*

l'étymologie (1953, Proof by Etymology)—made subtle and highly individual contributions to the essay. And Maurice Blanchot's meditations, beginning with his analyses in *False Step*, have taken the form of a mystique of negation.

But the essay is normally associated with creative activity that is secondary to the writing of novels, poetry, and plays. Are there important writers in our period since 1945 concerned solely with reflection and analysis?

Before World War II Alain (1868–1951, pseudonym of Émile Auguste Chartier) and Julien Benda (1867–1965) had brilliantly incarnated the literature of ideas. Alain was more of a philosopher, but a philosopher of everyday experience; in each of the short informal essays he called *propos* he studied the nature of things, writing in a fragmentary, discontinuous style. Julien Benda was more of a polemicist, but pursued a mathematically rigorous style of argument. Both Alain and Benda belonged to a rationalist and humanist tradition of clear and precise thought. They had reservations about the artistic experimentation of the period, with its taste for exploring the unconscious; but in other respects they were forward-looking men, involved with the political problems of the times. The postwar existentialist vogue overshadowed their last work, which appeared after 1945. Alain, however, through his position as professor, and Benda, through the sheer strength of his polemics, did continue to exercise an influence which can still be seen, especially among independent and unaligned thinkers.

Very far from their spirit was Jean Grenier's (1898–1970) singular, almost anachronistic mind; his writing and thought went against the grain of the century. Above all else, Grenier denounced the twentieth century for making a religion of history. Before World War II, at the very moment when the conflict between democracy and fascism was bringing intellectuals to see the need for political commitment, Grenier rejected, in *Essai sur l'esprit d'orthodoxie* (1938, Essay on the Spirit of Orthodoxy), all forms of collective thinking or action. In *L'existence malheureuse* (1957, The Misfortune of Existence) he reappraised Hegelianism and history's justification of contingency and evil. History, in Grenier's eyes, was no more than a bad dream: only truth was eternal. For Grenier, the revelation had already taken place: thus, the classics are more worthwhile models than contemporary intellectual and artistic experiments.

For Grenier, history was only the outward manifestation of a more fundamental evil of a metaphysical kind, namely *limitation*. How can one live without limitation, amputation? Although Grenier's problem, like the existentialists', was that of freedom (and of course he was the mentor of Camus, who willingly recognized his debt to Grenier), he was not thereby committed to an existentialist solution. For existentialism sees in freedom the opportunity of choice, responsibility, and the risk of practical action; like Marxism, it encloses us in a fragmentary and irreversible sequence of events, except for the element of personal decision. Like Gide in this respect, Grenier saw the great vital issue as the agony of choice between different possibilities: his fundamental indecision was due not to a character defect but to an awareness of the damaging and arbitrary nature of choice.

Consequently, the best use of freedom is not to choose, as Grenier showed in *Le choix* (1941, Choice) and *En-*

tretiens sur le bon usage de la liberté (1948, Discussions on the Proper Use of Freedom). Only indifference gives completeness. Only inaction, as Hinduism and eastern philosophy know, puts one in contact with being. Perhaps it was in *Les grèves* (1957, The Beaches), a fine book that is not as well known as it should be, that Grenier best expressed his ideas in a form that was half narration, half meditation. Discreet, soft-spoken, muted, a little distant, but elegant, rich, and supple, Grenier's work was a fine example of a bridge built between literature and philosophical meditation.

Grenier and Brice Parain (1897–1971) had some points in common: they belonged to the same generation; the writings of both men are little known or understood; both challenged the century's idolization of history and infection by the Hegelian dialectic. Like Grenier Parain experienced a solitude that he, too, described in his intellectual autobiography, *De fil en aiguille* (1960, Little by Little). But unlike Grenier, Parain did not seek solitude: he made every effort to join forces with others. He tried out the experience of communication in a practical way, by participating in the collective movements of the period: communism, surrealism, existentialism. But, seeing communication only in truth, he met falsehood everywhere. Just as nationalistic heroism (he fought in World War I, an experience that left deep marks) deceives us by taking no account of suffering, so surrealism deceives by pretending to alter life but simply talking, communism deceives by sacrificing the present to the future, the means to a questionable end, and existentialism deceives in offering man a pride that cannot save him from despair. What is the source of these lies? For Parain, one had to return to the origins, to the conditions of a common accord, which are the principles of thought and language. For thought is given us by speech; and language holds the key to communication. Giving names to things is the "first judgment," the "decisive moment of perception."

Parain's living quest for relationships thus resulted in a meditation on language which extended from his first essays, those in *Recherche sur la nature et les fonctions du langage* (1942, Research into the Nature and Functions of Language), through his last. Language contains a rule of truth (this was the message of Plato that Aristotle had falsified) which opens the road toward transcendence. For, according to Parain, the meaning of our contemporary deceits and disorders is clear: mankind needs a kind of religion. Parain's hesitant, stumbling, stubborn phrases have, rather like Péguy's, the moving gravity of an uncompromising quest.

Roger Caillois (born 1913), of a later generation, has also been hostile to the idols of the time. Caillois's style is brilliant, and his concerns various. Abstract vehemence, an entirely cerebral passion, and a dry fervor have sustained the work of one of France's most gifted stylists. But Caillois is concerned with knowledge and is not satisfied with mere words. Early in his career, in *Le mythe et l'homme* (1938, Myth and Man), he poured forth, in some disorder, a mass of penetrating sociological insights that all tended to challenge society; he examined our "critical" society, while longing and hoping for an "organic" society in which human communion could be established. He shared with his colleagues at the Collège de Sociologie, and with the surrealists, a longing for the mythic and the sacred.

Caillois's critique of society has encompassed a critique of art: he denounced art's innate dishonesty in *Procès intellectuel de l'art* (1936, An Intellectual Trial of Art) and its contemporary state of confusion in *Les impostures de la poésie* (1945, The Deceits of Poetry) and *Babel* (1948, Babel). But a book like *Le rocher de Sisyphe* (1946, The Rock of Sisyphus) had quite different roots: the war, which nearly resulted in an order far worse than the liberals' disorder, persuaded Caillois that everything could not be flatly rejected. A philosophy of civilization as human effort separated from nature allowed him both to continue his criticism and to reject rash experimentation. The essays of this period were marred, however, by a tendency toward special pleading, angry indictment, and turgidity.

In *Les jeux et les hommes* (1958, Games and Men) Caillois successfully returned to sociological analysis; and *Méduse et cie* (1960, Medusa & Co.), *Esthétique généralisée* (1962, Generalized Aesthetic), and *L'écriture des pierres* (1969, The Writing of the Stones) extended his meditations to take in the patterns of nature, whose crystals and plants also give us an example of orderliness. Caillois has thus stayed faithful to his ethical concerns, namely, to find those laws that, in every domain, construct and are hostile to all forms of disorganization.

Émile M. Cioran (born 1911), who moved to France from Rumania in 1937, rapidly established himself as one of France's best essayists with *Précis de décomposition* (1949, Summary of Decomposition), *Syllogisme de l'amertume* (1952, Syllogisms of Bitterness), *La tentation d'exister* (1956, The Temptation to Exist), and *La chute dans le temps* (1964, The Fall into Time). Cioran has written with clarity and precision, and with an intellectual agility that recalls Valéry.

But beneath, Cioran's crystal flickers with a desperate flame: a somber exaltation shatters and tarnishes it. Cioran's sociology is lyric and touching. He has investigated and questioned the twentieth century, the nations of the world, the Jews, Russia, Rumania, France, and conflicting political creeds. But his analysis has been carried out with anger and anguish; the syllogisms of bitterness find it hard to organize their throbbing and agonized material. Cioran's work is a painful confession: a wounded, sadomasochistic sensibility directs, but also blinds, his thought. He feels mortally wounded, and he excels in seizing on symptoms of decomposition and decadence. He is at once the wound and the knife.

And yet Cioran said, "The word 'no' enrages me." His destructive rage has sought its outer limit, its point of resistance. And the will to exist still survives in him. Nonetheless, like Nietzsche, he sees life and truth as opposites; he aspires to a life that cannot be his, which is denied him by the power of his own mind. Yet his works, the products of a destructive conscience, seem finally to negate negation, like acts of a theoretical hope, of a redeeming illusion, like the search for a compromise with what he calls "the nonevidence of living."

Essayists like Cioran, Caillois, and Parain have created an œuvre of impressive weight and achievement, book after book. Other essayists are important mainly for one or two isolated works. For example, Denis de Rougemont's (born 1906), singularly important contribution has been the prewar *L'amour et l'occident* (1936, Love and the West), which he revised in 1956. His postwar work has not had the same power. Thierry Maulnier, who made a reputation with brilliant essays of literary criticism—*Introduction à la poésie française* (1939, Introduction to French Poetry), *Lecture de Phèdre* (1943, An Interpretation of Phedre)—now rarely writes anything except newspaper editorials. Jules Monnerot (born 1908), connected with the Collège de Sociologie, published two major essays immediately after the war: *La poésie moderne et le sacré* (1945, Modern Poetry and the Sacred) and *Les faits sociaux ne sont pas des choses* (1946, Social Facts Are Not Things). But from *Sociologie du communisme* (1949, Sociology of Communism) onward, his militancy overcame his thoughtfulness. Wladimir Weidlé (born 1895) remains important mainly for *Les abeilles d'Aristée* (1936, 1954, The Bees of Aristaeus), one of the most profound meditations on the present destiny of art.

Rather than continue with a list of the important single essays of the last few decades, it would be more helpful to sketch the main directions the essay has taken. Assuming that creative literature can be reduced to certain currents, such trends are even more clearly evident in the literature of reflection.

Two major themes have recurred in the essay during the last twenty-five years: a questioning of language, and a challenging of society. Contemporary thought has not found new problems, but it has certainly shed new light upon the old ones, and it has adopted different approaches. Immediately after the war, the climate was existentialist, and the outlook both romantic and political. Existence, lived in anguish and hope, was the central concern: man sought reasons for existing and a means for acting; he sought values and purposes.

Sartre was in the forefront of those who pleaded for a committed literature. Now the climate has changed, and he has rejected literature itself, considering it the expression of a culture and society he repudiates. But, unlike some younger writers, he did not erase the slate. *The Idiot of the Family* proved that he is still primarily interested in understanding the individual, and, as his political activity proves, in being a man, not an intellect divorced from human concerns.

Similarly, Maurice Merleau-Ponty has continually investigated the concrete problems of existence: his inquiry into perception in *Phénoménologie de la perception* (1948, Phenomenology of Perception) sought the link between knowledge and the human organism, the point of unison. And, going beyond the narrowly political outlook of *Humanisme et terreur* (1947, Humanism and Terror)—to which he bid farewell in *Les aventures de la dialectique* (1955, The Adventures of Dialectic)—in *Éloge de la philosophie* (1953, In Praise of Philosophy) he sought the meaning of man's action in history.

In Praise of Philosophy rejected humanism as "human chauvinism"; but Merleau-Ponty nonetheless still holds to the sort of humanism espoused through Christian and personalist existentialism by Emmanuel Mounier (1905–1950), founder of the review *Esprit*, to the humanism of Henri Lefebvre's (born 1901) Marxism, and to the humanism in Raymond Aron's conservative liberalism. Moreover, Merleau-Ponty's meditations on language—an interest he shared with Paulhan, Parain, and Blanchot—have been directed toward language's immediate uses.

All the writers I have discussed so far have been essayists in the traditional sense—writers who interpret general concepts or even scientific data so as to give their personal answers to urgent questions. Unlike them, the "new essayists" seem more like *scientists*, or, more precisely, explorers of human sciences that are in the process of creation. They had based their authority on the supposedly anonymous and objective theoretical apparatus of linguistics, ethnology, semeiology, and psychoanalysis. If their forerunners challenged and debunked the illusions of consciousness, they still did so in the name of consciousness, by a subjective, existential act. But now the very subject, the source of this mystification, is being debunked.

The decisive break came with the rejection of the Cartesian *cogito* to which the thought of Sartre, Camus, and Merleau-Ponty was still to some extent related. In ethnology, this break was embodied in the work of Claude Levi-Strauss, who wanted structuralism to eliminate all ethnocentrism. In psychoanalysis, Jacques Lacan formulated an *anti-cogito* that delivered him from all psychology ("I think where I am not; therefore, I am where I think not").

In semeiology, there have been a number of attempts, such as those of Roland Barthes, Louis Althusser, and Jacques Derrida, to propose *readings* of phenomena, fashion, society, economy, and writing itself. In other words, they have tried to eliminate first of all the illusory meanings which obscure the "signifieds" that are to be catalogued, and to eliminate even the illusion of meaning. Their object is to go from the superficial surface of the discourse (which corresponds to reality no better than our picture of reality corresponds to physical reality) back to the underlying discourse. The text of history, said Althusser, "is not a text in which a voice (the logos) speaks, but the inaudible and unreadable notation of the effects of a structure of structures. . . ."

Behind this epistemological revolution lie Marx, Freud, and Nietzsche, three masters of suspicion, and also the linguistics of Ferdinand de Saussurian (1857–1913). Saussurian showed that the study of speech presupposes the study of language. This revolution in thought emphasized not the meanings of speech but the supportive system of language and its code, thus showing us that "meaning is phenomenal" and that "behind all meaning there is a nonmeaning" (Lévi-Strauss).

If these writers have sought to pass beyond immediate appearances to a structural reality, as the natural sciences do, should we not classify them as scientific? And are they not out of place in a literary survey? Yet, their influence on literature should be enough to make us take note. On the one hand, structuralism expresses an attitude, a choice that presents itself both in literature and in art: if direct knowledge is denounced, it is because the direct existence of the individual, of society and of culture, is rejected. The chilly anonymity of science expresses a rejection of all forms of personal experience, a deep-seated antihumanism. Thus, the only pure activity, the only one that does not turn the mind into its detestable accomplice, consists in inscribing, on a slate wiped clean of existence and its meanings, those structures that have no meaning save that they are there. Yet, on the other hand, the human sciences are still far from attaining the objective status of the natural sciences; and they have in them much that is prescientific and consequently leaves considerable room for creativity and imagination. Both scientific immaturity and original personal points of view therefore keep the works of these writers inside the category of literature.

Thus, whether they like it or not, the anti-Cartesian essayists are part of literature and can be compared stylistically to other writers. Jacques Lacan in his *Écrits* (1966, Writings) has shown a preciosity reminiscent of Stephane Mallarmé (1842–1898) and even of the Spaniard Luis de Gongora. Roland Barthes revealed a felicitous style and imagination in *Mythologies* (1965, Mythologies), *Système de la mode* (1967, The System of Fashion), and *L'empire des signes* (1969, The Empire of Signs). Louis Althusser, in *Lire le Capital* (1965, Reading "Capital") and *Pour Marx* (1965, For Marx), and Jacques Derrida, in *L'écriture et la différence* (1967, Writing and Difference), both used inspired, muted tones, whispering on the brink of mystery, allowing words to guide their footsteps, resembling Bataille or Blanchot.

There are of course other works, such as Michel Foucault's *Les mots et les choses* (1966, Words and Things), with an equally great influence on contemporary writing, but which definitely belong not to literature but to philosophy and the philosophy of history, or to science proper, like the work of Claude Lévi-Strauss. But Lévi-Strauss's *Tristes tropiques* (1955, Sad Tropics) is itself literature. And the impressive display of rigorous analysis in his *Mythologiques* (1964–72, Mythologics) has the architecture of a musical composition.

Histories of literature have always contained a chapter on literary criticism—generally a modest chapter, for literary criticism revolves around imaginative literature. But today, it seems that much literature revolves around criticism; the argument over the "new criticism" made nearly as much ink flow as did those about the "new novel," or the "new theater." Since literary creation is a product of the intellect, why should literary criticism not be its equal, and even its model? It is as if the work of art suffers from a sort of original sin—its physical existence—from which criticism can deliver it, by extracting its structure or, as Georges Poulet (born 1914), who has openly claimed the superiority of criticism, would put it, its *cogito*.

Until lately criticism followed in creation's footsteps; it was the work's echo and evaluation. Today, criticism says what the work, whether classic or contemporary, did not know it had said; and it extracts from its awareness a whole theory of literature. Previously, the best critic was the one who was able to detect quality before the passing of time conferred immortality, as well as the one who could summon up a writing talent of his own in the service of this function. Today, the most outstanding critic is considered to be the one who uses the most precise conceptual apparatus to formulate his theory. Consequently, the major tendency of contemporary criticism is not toward talent or aesthetic choice but toward different systems of interpretation.

This shift has resulted in a break with traditions of literary scholarship and criticism, the tradition of Gustave Lanson (1857–1934) and Albert Thibaudet (1874–1936). Most critics no longer seek to establish particular facts or to explain, rather they try to disclose general laws and structures; even studies of individual writers and works seek the general rule behind the particular instance. Contemporary thinking universally suspects appearances and dislikes diversity; the wide range of Thibaudet's comparisons is over and done with. Although Raymond Picard (born 1917), in *Nouvelle critique ou nouvelle imposture?* (1965, New Criticism or New Fraud?) demonstrated, in the name of the tradition of university scholarship, that Roland Barthes's *Sur Racine* (1963, On Racine) was historically inconsequential, the tendency of our age is to favor Barthes's reply in *Critique et verité* (1966, Criticism and Truth).

There also exists today a kind of criticism we may call "existential." Critics of this school believe that a work's true essence is to be found in the experiences of its author. Those experiences occur at a deep level, however, without the author's being fully aware of them; such criticism has nothing to do with biographical anecdotes. Proust, in some passages of *La prisonnière* (1923, The Captive) was a forerunner of this method. And the outstanding works of Gaston Bachelard (1884–1962), from *La psychanalyse du feu* (1938, The Psychoanalysis of Fire) to *La poétique de l'espace* (1957), The Poetics of Space), in a sense founded this school of criticism. Marcel Raymond's (born 1897) *De Baudelaire au surréalisme* (1933, 1947, From Baudelaire to Surrealism) was a key work of existential criticism.

Georges Poulet brought to this type of criticism a Kantian slant: with inspired subtlety he has analyzed the author's basic *cogito*, his relationship to the fundamental categories of space and time. His admirable books include *Études sur le temps humain* (1950, Studies in Human Time); *Le distance intérieure* (1952, The Interior Distance), *Les métamorphoses du cercle* (1961, The Metamorphoses of the Circle).

Jean-Pierre Richard (born 1922) is the empiricist of

this school. Within the general pattern he seeks the most precise instances, in such work as *Littérature et sensation* (1954, Literature and Sensation), *Poésie et profondeur* (1955, Poetry and Profundity), *L'univers imaginaire de Mallarmé* (1961, Mallarmé's Imaginative Universe). Existential criticism has often been inspired by psychoanalysis; a good example was Charles Mauron's (born 1899) *Introduction à la psychocritique* (1963, Introduction to Psychocriticism). But Sartre, in works like *Baudelaire* (1947, Baudelaire) and *The Idiot of the Family*, made a healthy distinction between psychoanalysis proper and existential psychoanalysis, insisting on the human capacity for a choice and a purpose that are not necessarily determined by a childhood trauma.

The last ten years have been even more dominated by a formalist criticism in which the literary work is interpreted not by the ideology or the hidden life of its author but by the latent systems of language. Seeking patterns in the language of fiction and poetry, Roland Barthes, Gérard Genette (born 1930), Tavetan Todorov (born 1935), and Jean Cohen (born 1936) have worked toward a formalization of the theory of literature. They no longer see style as a "self-sufficient language," dependent on the writer's obsessions and drive toward originality. Instead, language for them is anonymous. They do not analyze works, but theorize about what makes works into literature; the tendency is to write a history of texts divorced from authors and dates.

Barthes passed from thematic and "mythological" criticism of *Michelet par lui-même* (1954, Michelet by Himself) and *On Racine* to the semeiological point of view. Even in his first work he was semeiological, but the symbols he elicited were merely deceptive appearances. The true practice of semeiology involves discovering consistent literary patterns behind stylistic variations, moving away from the superficial meaning toward a meaning that is not relative—in other words, toward the irreversible basic structure.

The postwar period has also had a sociological criticism, usually Marxist. It has been furthered by such critics as Lucien Goldmann (1913–1970), a disciple of Lukács, in works like *Le dieu caché* (1955, The Hidden God). Sociological criticism depends on the concept of a *world view*; the work is the expression of the outlook of a particular group.

These different schools of criticism tend to be mutually exclusive. Sartre, however, has sought to integrate existential and sociological approaches. And Georges Blin (born 1917), in his monumental works on Stendhal, and Jean Starobinski (born 1920), in a succession of masterly books—*Jean-Jacques Rousseau: La transparence et l'obstacle* (1957, Jean-Jacques Rousseau: Transparency and Obstacle), *Montesquieu par lui-même* (1953, Montesquieu by Himself) and the series of studies in *L'oeil vivant* (1961–70, The Living Eye)—have both drawn on all these approaches, without overlooking historical accuracy or the work's own reality as an individual phenomenon that can also be enjoyed. This position has, of course, rubbed against the grain of current intellectual fashion, which sees in "enjoyment" a gastronomic habit connected with the much-challenged consumer society.

As a whole, contemporary criticism has sought to go beyond literature and become science. But the frontier has not yet been crossed, and so we still fortunately find ourselves within literature. So long as scientific objectivity is not attained, so long as argument and controversy continue, so long will an appreciable margin be left for the writer's talent and imagination. Barthes's distinction between language and writing has been a two-edged weapon: he himself has used the self-sufficient language of the writer. Espousing the *cogito* of a work, Georges Poulet has depicted himself as much as he does his subject. And Blanchot's highly influential criticism, through which the book to be analyzed was merely a pretext for his own meditation on speech, preserved the tone of his own fiction—the tone of inspiration.

If modern criticism, although still part of literature because of its own uncertainties, seeks to step outside it, this wish merely expresses a fundamental tendency of literature itself. Turning its back on diversity, on the sense, on the idiosyncracies of history and the individual, contemporary criticism was accompanied by and justified literature's withdrawal from life. Because literature has moved away from creation into the realm of ideas, criticism has begun to look like literature's goal. But this goal, if it were ever attained, would mean the end of literature.

BIBLIOGRAPHY

ENGLISH TRANSLATIONS

The following is a list of published English translations of the works mentioned in this book. Where more than one translation exists, the most recent American translation has been chosen. This list includes only work-for-work translations; many individual poems or stories from collections mentioned have appeared in English in different combinations.

Achard, Marcel. *Auprès de ma blonde* as *I Know My Love*. New York, 1952
————. *Patate* as *Rollo*. London, 1960
Adamov, Arthur. *Paolo Paoli* as *Paolo Paoli*. London, 1960
————. *Le ping-pong* as *Ping Pong*. New York, 1959
————. *Le professeur Taranne* as *Professor Taranne*. In *Four Modern French Comedies*. New York, 1960
Althusser, Louis. *Pour Marx* as *For Marx*. New York, 1969
Althusser, Louis and Étienne Balibar. *Lire le Capital* as *Reading "Capital."* New York, 1971
Anouilh, Jean. *L'alouette* as *The Lark*. In *Five Plays*, vol. 2. New York, 1959
————. *Antigone* as *Antigone*. In *Five Plays*, vol. 1. New York, 1958
————. *Ardèle, ou la marguerite* as *Ardele*. In *Five Plays*, vol. 2. New York, 1959
————. *Becket, ou l'honneur de Dieu* as *Becket, or the Honor of God*. New York, 1960
————. *Cher Antoine* as *Dear Antoine*. New York, 1971
————. *La foire d'empoigne* as *Catch as Catch Can*. In *Seven Plays*, vol. 3. New York, 1967
————. *L'hermine* as *The Ermine*. In *Five Plays*, vol. 1. New York, 1958

————. *Pauvre Bitos* as *Poor Bitos*. New York, 1964
————. *La sauvage* as *Restless Heart*. In *Five Plays*, vol. 2. New York, 1959
————. *La valse des toréadors* as *The Waltz of the Toreadors*. New York, 1957
————. *Le voyageur sans bagage* as *Traveler without Luggage*. In *Seven Plays*, vol. 3. New York, 1967
Apollinaire, Guillaume. *Les mamelles de Tirésias* as *The Breasts of Tiresias*. In Michael Benedikt and George Wellwarth, eds., *Modern French Theatre*. New York, 1966
————. *Zone* as *Zone*. In *Alcools*. Berkeley, Cal., 1965
Aragon, Louis. *Aurélien* as *Aurélien*. New York, 1947
————. *Les beaux quartiers* as *Residential Quarter*. New York, 1938
————. *Les cloches de Bâle* as *The Bells of Basel*. New York, 1936
————. *Le paysan de Paris* as *Nightwalker*. Englewood Cliffs, N.J., 1970
————. *La semaine sainte* as *Holy Week*. New York, 1961
————. *Les voyageurs de l'impériale* as *Passengers of Destiny*. London, 1949
Arrabal, Fernando. *Le cimetière des voitures* as *The Automobile Graveyard*. In *The Automobile Graveyard, and The Two Executioners*. New York, 1960
Artaud, Antonin. *Au pays des Tarahumaras* as *Concerning a Journey to the Land of the Tarahumaras*. In *Antonin Artaud Anthology*. San Francisco, 1965
————. *Les Cenci* as *The Cenci*. New York, 1970
————. *L'ombilic des limbes* as *Umbilical Limbo*. In *Collected Works*, vol. 1. London, 1968
————. *Le théâtre et son double* as *The Theater and Its Double*. New York, 1958
————. *Van Gogh, le suicidé de la société* as *Van Gogh: The Man Suicided by Society*. In *Antonin Artaud Anthology*. San Francisco, 1965
Aymé, Marcel. *Clérambard* as *Clérambard*. In *Four Modern French Comedies*. New York, 1960
Bachelard, Gaston. *La poétique de l'espace* as *The Poetics of Space*. New York, 1964
————. *La psychanalyse du feu* as *The Psychoanalysis of Fire*. Boston, 1964

Barthes, Roland. *Mythologies* as *Mythologies*. New York, 1972
———. *Sur Racine* as *On Racine*. New York, 1964
Bataille, Georges. *Lascaux, ou la naissance de l'art* as *Lascaux, or the Birth of Art*. Lausanne, 1955
———. *Manet* as *Manet*. New York, 1955
Beauvoir, Simone de. *Le deuxième sexe* as *The Second Sex*. New York, 1953
———. *La force de l'âge* as *The Prime of Life*. Cleveland, 1962
———. *L'invitée* as *She Came to Stay*. Cleveland, 1954
———. *Les Mandarins* as *The Mandarins*. New York, 1960
———. *Mémoires d'une jeune fille rangée* as *Memoirs of a Dutiful Daughter*. Cleveland, 1959
———. *Le sang des autres* as *The Blood of Others*. New York, 1948
———. *Tous les hommes sont mortels* as *All Men Are Mortal*. Cleveland, 1955
———. *La vieillesse* as *The Coming of Age*. New York, 1972
Beckett, Samuel. *Comment c'est* as *How It Is*. New York, 1964
———. *En attendant Godot* as *Waiting for Godot*. New York, 1954
———. *Fin de partie* as *Endgame*. In *Endgame/Act without Words*. New York, 1958
———. *Happy Days*. New York, 1961
———. *L'innommable* as *The Unnamable*. In *Three Novels*. New York, 1965
———. *Malone meurt* as *Malone Dies*. In *Three Novels*. New York, 1965
———. *Molloy* as *Molloy*. In *Three Novels*. New York, 1965
Bernanos, Georges. *Dialogues des Carmélites* as *The Fearless Heart*. London, 1952
———. *La France contre les robots* as *Tradition of Freedom*. London, 1950
———. *Journal d'un curé de campagne* as *The Diary of a Country Priest*. New York, 1962
———. *Lettre aux Anglais* as *Plea for Liberty: Letters to the English, the Americans, the Europeans*. New York, 1944
———. *Un mauvais rêve* as *Night is Darkest*. London, 1953
———. *Monsieur Ouine* as *The Open Mind*. London, 1945
———. *Sous le soleil de Satan* as *Under the Sun of Satan*. New York, 1949

Billetdoux, François. *Tchin-tchin* as *Tchin-Tchin*. In *Two Plays*. New York, 1964

———. *Va donc chez Törpe* as *Chez Torpe*. In *Two Plays*. New York, 1964

Bonnefoy, Yves. *Du mouvement et de l'immobilité de Douve* as *On the Motion and Immobility of Douve*. Athens, Ohio, 1968

Bosco, Henri. *Le mas Théotime* as *Farm in Provence*. Garden City, N. Y., 1947

Breton, André. *Ode à Charles Fourier* as *Ode to Charles Fourier*. London, 1969

Butor, Michel. *Degrés* as *Degrees*. New York, 1961

———. *L'emploi du temps* as *Passing Time*. In *Passing Time, and A Change of Heart: Two Novels*. New York, 1969

———. *Mobile* as *Mobile*. New York, 1963

———. *La modification* as *A Change of Heart*. In *Passing Time, and A Change of Heart: Two Novels*. New York, 1969

———. *Le roman comme recherche* as *The Novel as Research*. In *Inventory*. New York, 1968

———. *6,810,000 litres d'eau par seconde* as *Niagara*. Chicago, 1969

Caillois, Roger. *Les jeux et les hommes* as *Man, Play, and Games*. New York, 1961

———. *Méduse et cie* as *The Mask of Medusa*. New York, 1964

Camus, Albert. *Caligula* as *Caligula*. In *Caligula, and Three Other Plays*. New York, 1958

———. *La chute* as *The Fall*. New York, 1957

———. *L'état de siège* as *State of Siege*. In *Caligula, and Three Other Plays*. New York, 1958

———. *L'étranger* as *The Stranger*. New York, 1946

———. *L'exil et le royaume* as *Exile and the Kingdom*. New York, 1958

———. *Les justes* as *The Just Assassins*. In *Caligula, and Three Other Plays*. New York, 1958

———. *Le malentendu* as *The Misunderstanding*. In *Caligula, and Three Other Plays*. New York, 1958

———. *Le mythe de Sisyphe* as *The Myth of Sisyphus*. New York, 1955

———. *La peste* as *The Plague*. New York, 1948

———. *L'homme révolté* as *The Rebel: An Essay on Man in Revolt*. New York, 1954

Céline, Louis-Ferdinand. *D'un château l'autre* as *Castle to Castle*. New York, 1968
———. *Mort à credit* as *Death on the Installment Plan*. New York, 1966
———. *Nord* as *North*. New York, 1972
———. *Voyage au bout de la nuit* as *Journey to the End of the Night*. New York, 1947
Césaire, Aimé. *Cahier d'un retour au pays natal* as *Return to My Native Land*. Baltimore, 1969
———. *Une saison au Congo* as *A Season in the Congo*. New York, 1969
Char, René. *Feuillets d'Hypos* as *Hypnos Waking*. New York, 1956
Cioran, Émile. *La chute dans le temps* as *The Fall into Time*. Chicago, 1970
———. *La tentation d'exister* as *The Temptation to Exist*. Chicago, 1968
Claudel, Paul. *L'histoire de Tobie et de Sara* as *Tobias and Sara*. In Richard Francis Hayes, ed., *Port-Royal, and Other Plays*. New York, 1962
———. *Le livre de Christophe Colomb* as *The Book of Christopher Columbus*. New Haven, Conn., 1930
———. *L'otage* as *The Hostage*. In *Three Plays*. Boston, 1945
———. *Partage de midi* as *Break of Noon*. In *Two Dramas*. Chicago, 1960
———. *Le soulier de satin* as *The Satin Slipper*. New Haven, Conn., 1931
———. *Tête d'or* as *Tête d'Or*. New Haven, Conn., 1919
———. *La ville* as *The City*. New Haven, Conn., 1920
Daumal, René. *Mont-Analogue* as *Mount Analogue*. San Francisco, 1968
Des Forêts, Louis-René. *Le bavard* as *The Bavard*. In *The Children's Room*. London, 1963
———. *La chambre des enfants* as *The Children's Room*. London, 1966
———. *Les mendiants* as *The Beggars*. London, 1949
Dubillard, Roland. *Naïves hirondelles* as *Naïves Hirondelles*. New York, 1968
Duras, Marguerite. *L'amante anglaise* as *L'Amante Anglaise*. New York, 1968

————. *Un barrage contre le Pacifique* as *The Sea Wall*. New York, 1967

————. *Détruire, dit-elle* as *Destroy, She Said*. New York, 1970

————. *Moderato cantabile* as *Moderato Cantabile*. In *Four Novels*. New York, 1965

————. *Les petits chevaux de Tarquinia* as *The Little Horses of Tarquinia*. London, 1960

————. *Le square* (novel) as *The Square*. In *Four Novels*. New York, 1965

————. *Le square* (play) as *The Square*. In *Three Plays*. London, 1967

Éluard, Paul. *Le dur désir de durer* as *Le Dur Désir de Durer*. New York, 1950

Gary, Romain. *Éducation européenne* as *A European Education*. New York, 1960

Gascar, Pierre. *Le temps des morts* as *The Season of the Dead*. In *Beasts and Men*. Boston, 1956

Genet, Jean. *Le balcon* as *The Balcony*. New York, 1960

————. *Les bonnes* as *The Maids*. In *The Maids and Deathwatch: Two Plays*. New York, 1954

————. *Journal du voleur* as *The Thief's Journal*. New York, 1964

————. *Miracle de la rose* as *Miracle of the Rose*. New York, 1966

————. *Les nègres* as *The Blacks*. New York, 1960

————. *Notre-Dame des Fleurs* as *Our Lady of the Flowers*. New York, 1963

Ghelderode, Michel de. *Fastes d'enfer* as *Chronicles of Hell*. In *Seven Plays*, vol. 1. New York, 1960

————. *Hop, signor!* as *Hop, Signor!* In *Seven Plays*, vol. 2. New York, 1964

Gide, André. *Corydon* as *Corydon*. New York, 1950

————. *Journal 1942–1949* as *The Journals of André Gide*, vol. 4: 1939–1949. New York, 1951

————. *Thésée* as *Theseus*. In *Two Legends: Oedipus and Theseus*. New York, 1950

Gide, André and Jean-Louis Barrault. *Le procès* as *The Trial*. New York, 1964

Giono, Jean. *Angelo* as *Angelo*. London, 1960.

————. *Le bonheur fou* as *The Straw Man*. New York, 1959

————. *Le chant du monde* as *The Song of the World*. New York, 1937

————. *Le hussard sur le toit* as *The Horseman on the Roof*. New York, 1966

Giraudoux, Jean. *La folle de Chaillot* as *The Madwoman of Chaillot*. New York, 1949

————. *La menteuse* as *Lying Woman*. New York, 1972

Goldmann, Lucien. *Le dieu caché* as *The Hidden God*. New York, 1964

Gracq, Julien. *Au château d'Argol* as *The Castle of Argol*. Norfolk, Conn, 1951

————. *Un balcon en forêt* as *Balcony in the Forest*. New York, 1959

————. *Un beau ténébreux* as *A Dark Stranger*. Norfolk, Conn., 1950

Green, Julien. *Moïra* as *Moira*. New York, 1951

————. *Sud* as *South*. In J. C. Trewin, ed., *Plays of the Year*, vol. 12. London, 1955

————. *Le voyageur sur la terre* as *The Pilgrim on Earth*. New York, 1929

Guilloux, Louis. *Le sang noir* as *Bitter Victory*. New York, 1938

Ionesco, Eugène. *Amédée, ou comment s'en débarrasser* as *Amédée, or How to Get Rid of It*. In *Three Plays*. New York, 1958

————. *La cantatrice chauve* as *The Bald Soprano*. In *Four Plays*. New York, 1958

————. *Les chaises* as *The Chairs*. In *Four Plays*. New York, 1958

————. *Jacques, ou la soumission* as *Jack, or. The Submission*. In *Four Plays*. New York, 1958

————. *Journal en miettes* as *Fragments of a Journal*. New York, 1968

————. *La leçon* as *The Lesson*. In *Four Plays*. New York, 1958

————. *Le piéton de l'air* as *A Stroll in the Air*. In *A Stroll in the Air & Frenzy for Two or More: Two Plays*. New York, 1968

————. *Le rhinocéros* as *Rhinoceros*. In *Rhinoceros, and Other Plays*. New York, 1960

————. *Le roi se meurt* as *Exit the King*. New York, 1968

————. *Tueur sans gages* as *The Killer*. In *The Killer, and Other Plays*. New York, 1960

Jarry, Alfred. *Ubu roi* as *King Ubu*. In Michael Benedikt and

George Wellwarth, eds., *Modern French Theatre*. New York, 1966

Jouve, Pierre Jean. *Le Don Juan de Mozart* as *Mozart's Don Juan*. London, 1957

———. *Ténèbre* as *An Idiom of Night*. Chicago, 1969

Klossowski, Pierre. *La révocation de l'Édit de Nantes* as *The Revocation of the Edict of Nantes*. In *Roberte Ce Soir/The Revocation of the Edict of Nantes*. New York, 1969

———. *Roberte, ce soir* as *Roberte Ce Soir* in *Roberte Ce Soir/ The Revocation of the Edict of Nantes*. New York, 1969

La Tour du Pin, Patrice de. *Une somme de poésie* as *The Dedicated Life in Poetry* and *The Correspondence of Laurent de Cayeux*. London, 1948

Laurent, Jacques. *Caroline chérie* as *Caroline Chérie*. New York, 1952

Le Clézio, J. M. G. *La fièvre* as *Fever*. New York, 1966

———. *Le procès-verbal* as *The Interrogation*. New York, 1964

———. *Terra amata* as *Terra Amata*. New York, 1969

Leduc, Violette. *La bâtarde* as *La Bâtarde*. New York, 1965

Leiris, Michel. *L'âge d'homme* as *Manhood*. In *Manhood, Preceded by The Autobiographer as Torero*. London, 1968

Lévi-Strauss, Claude. *Tristes tropiques* as *Tristes Tropiques*. New York, 1964

Mallet-Joris, Françoise. *Le rampart des béguines* as *Into the Labyrinth*. London, 1953

Malraux, André. *Antimémoires* as *Anti-Memoirs*. New York, 1968

———. *Les chênes qu'on abat* as *Felled Oaks*. New York, 1972

———. *La condition humaine* as *Man's Fate*. New York, 1936

———. *Les conquérants* as *The Conquerors*. New York, 1929

———. *L'espoir* as *Man's Hope*. New York, 1938

———. *La métamorphose des dieux* as *The Metamorphosis of the Gods*, vol. 1. Garden City, N. Y., 1960

———. *Les noyers de l'Altenburg* as *The Walnut Trees of Altenburg*. London, 1952

———. *Saturne* as *Saturn, an Essay on Goya*. New York, 1957

———. *Le temps du mépris* as *Days of Wrath*. New York, 1964

———. *La tentation de l'occident* as *The Temptation of the West*. New York, 1961

———. *La voie royale* as *The Royal Way*. New York, 1935

———. *Les voix du silence* as *The Voices of Silence*. New York, 1953

Marceau, Félicien. *L'œuf* as *The Egg*. London, 1958

Martin du Gard, Roger. *Les Thibaults* (parts 1–6 as *The Thibaults*. New York, 1939; *Les Thibaults* (parts 7–8) as *Summer 1914*. New York, 1941

Mauriac, François. *Un adolescent d'autrefois* as *Maltaverne*. New York, 1970

——. *Asmodée* as *Asmodée*. In Richard Francis Hayes, ed., *Port-Royal, and Other Plays*. New York, 1962.

——. *Le feu sur la terre* as *The River of Fire*. London, 1954

——. *Le nœud de vipères* as *Vipers' Tangle*. New York, 1947

Merle, Robert. *Week-end à Zuydcoote* as *Weekend at Dunkirk*. New York, 1951

Merleau-Ponty, Maurice. *Éloge de la philosophie* as *In Praise of Philosophy*. New York, 1963

——. *Humanisme et terreur* as *Humanism and Terror: An Essay on the Communist Problem*. Boston, 1969

——. *Phénoménologie de la perception* as *Phenomenology of Perception*. New York, 1962

Michaux, Henri. *Un barbare en Asie* as *A Barbarian in Asia*. Norfolk, Conn., 1949

——. *Misérable miracle* as *Miserable Miracle: Mescaline*. San Francisco, 1967

Michel, Georges. *La promenade du dimanche* as *The Sunday Walk*. London, 1968

Mohrt, Michel. *La prison maritime* as *Mariners' Prison*. New York, 1963

Monnerot, Jules. *Sociologie du communisme* as *Sociology and Psychology of Communism*. Boston, 1953

Montherlant, Henry de. *Le cardinal d'Espagne* as *The Cardinal of Spain*. In J. C. Trewin, ed., *Plays of the Year*, Vol. 37. London, 1969

——. *Le chaos et la nuit* as *Chaos and Night*. New York, 1964

——. *La guerre civile* as *Civil War*. In Robert Baldick, ed., *Theatre of War*. Harmondsworth, England, 1967

——. *Les jeunes filles* as *The Girls: A Tetralogy of Novels*. New York, 1968

——. *La reine morte* as *Queen after Death*. In *The Master of Santiago, and Four Other Plays*. New York, 1951

——. *La rose de sable* as *Desert Love*. New York, 1957

——. *Le songe* as *The Dream*. New York, 1963

Obaldia, René de. *Du vent dans les branches de sassafras* as *Wind in the Branches of the Sassafras.* In *Modern International Drama,* vol. 1, no. 2, March, 1968

Ollier, Claude. *Le maintien de l'ordre* as *Law and Order.* New York, 1971

Picard, Raymond. *Nouvelle critique ou nouvelle imposture?* as *New Criticism or New Fraud?* Pullman, Wash., 1969

Pieyre de Mandiargues, André. *Le lis de mer* as *The Girl beneath the Lion.* New York, 1958

————. *La marge* as *The Margin.* New York, 1969

————. *La motocyclette* as *The Motorcycle.* New York, 1965

Pinget, Robert. *L'inquisitoire* as *The Inquisitory.* New York, 1967

————. *Lettre morte* as *Dead Letter.* In *Plays,* vol. 1. New York, 1966

Ponge, Francis. *Le savon* as *Soap.* London, 1969

Poulet, Georges. *La distance intérieure* as *The Interior Distance.* Baltimore, 1959

————. *Études sur le temps humain* as *Studies in Human Time.* Baltimore, 1956

————. *Les métamorphoses du cercle* as *The Metamorphoses of the Circle.* Baltimore, 1967

Prévert, Jacques. *Paroles* as *Selections from Paroles.* San Francisco, 1958

Proust, Marcel. *La prisonnière* as *The Captive.* New York, 1929

Queneau, Raymond. *Le chiendent* as *The Bark-Tree.* London, 1968

————. *Exercices de style* as *Exercises in Style.* New York, 1958

————. *Les fleurs bleues* as *The Blue Flowers.* New York, 1967

————. *Loin de Rueil* as *The Skin of Dreams.* Norfolk, Conn., 1948

————. *Pierrot mon ami* as *Pierrot: A Novel.* London, 1950

————. *Zazie dans le métro* as *Zazie.* New York, 1960

Raymond, Marcel. *De Baudelaire au surréalisme* as *From Baudelaire to Surrealism.* New York, 1949

Robbe-Grillet, Alain. *Dans le labyrinthe* as *In the Labyrinth.* New York, 1960

————. *Les gommes* as *The Erasers.* New York, 1964

————. *Instantanés* as *Snapshots.* New York, 1968

————. *La jalousie* as *Jealousy.* New York, 1959

————. *La maison de rendez-vous* as *La Maison de Rendez-vous.* New York, 1966

————. *Nature, humanisme et tragédie* as *Nature, Humanism,*

Tragedy. In *For a New Novel: Essays on Fiction*. New York, 1965
——. *Projet pour une révolution à New York* as *Project for a Revolution in New York*. New York, 1972
——. *Une voie pour le roman futur* as *A Future for the Novel*. In *For a New Novel: Essays on Fiction*. New York, 1965
——. *Le voyeur* as *The Voyeur*. New York, 1967
Roblès, Emmanuel. *Montserrat* as *Montserrat*. New York, 1950
Rougement, Denis de. *L'amour et l'occident* as *Love in the Western World*, rev. ed. New York, 1956
Rousseau, Jean-Jacques. *Julie, ou la nouvelle Héloise* as *Julie, or the New Eloise*. University Park, Pa., 1968
Rousset, David. *L'univers concentrationnaire* as *The Other Kingdom*. New York, 1947
Roussin, André. *La petite hutte* as *The Little Hut*. New York, 1952
Roy, Jules. *La vallée heureuse* as *The Happy Valley*. London, 1952
Sagan, Françoise. *Bonjour tristesse* as *Bonjour Tristesse*. New York, 1955
——. *Un certain sourire* as *A Certain Smile*. New York, 1956
Saint-Exupéry, Antoine de. *Citadelle* as *The Wisdom of the Sands*. New York, 1950
——. *Pilote de guerre* as *Flight to Arras*. New York, 1942
——. *Un sens à la vie* as *A Sense of Life*. New York, 1965
——. *Terre des hommes* as *Wind, Sand, and Stars*. New York, 1949
——. *Vol de nuit* as *Night Flight*. New York, 1932
Saint-John Perse. *Amers* as *Seamarks*. New York, 1958
——. *Anabase* as *Anabasis*, new ed. London, 1959
——. *Chronique* as *Chronique*. New York, 1961
——. *Éloges* as *Éloges*. In *Eloges, and Other Poems*. New York, 1956
——. *Exil* as *Exile*. In *Exile, and Other Poems*. New York, 1949
——. *Neiges* as *Snows*. In *Exile, and Other Poems*. New York, 1949
——. *Oiseaux* as *Birds*. New York, 1966
——. *Pluies* as *Rains*. In *Exile, and Other Poems*. New York, 1949
——. *Vents* as *Winds*, 2d ed. New York, 1961

Sarraute, Nathalie. *Entre la vie et la mort* as *Between Life and Death*. New York, 1969

———. *L'ère du soupçon* as *The Age of Suspicion*. New York, 1963

———. *Les fruits d'or* as *The Golden Fruits*. New York, 1964

———. *Martereau* as *Martereau: A Novel*. New York, 1959.

———. *Le mensonge* as *The Lie*. In *Silence, and The Lie*. London, 1969

———. *Le planétarium* as *The Planetarium*. New York, 1960

———. *Portrait d'un inconnu* as *Portrait of a Man Unknown*. New York, 1958

———. *Le silence* as *Silence*. In *Silence, and The Lie*. London, 1969.

———. *Tropismes* as *Tropisms*. New York, 1967

Sartre, Jean-Paul. *L'âe de raison* as *The Age of Reason*. New York, 1947

———. *Baudelaire* as *Baudelaire*. Norfolk, Conn., 1950

———. *Critique de la raison dialectique* as *Search for a Method*. New York, 1963

———. *Le Diable et le bon Dieu* as *The Devil & the Good Lord*. In *The Devil & the Good Lord, and Two Other Plays*. New York, 1960

———. *L'être et le néant* as *Being and Nothingness*. New York, 1956

———. *Huis clos* as *No Exit*. In *No Exit & The Flies*. New York, 1947

———. *L'imaginaire* as *The Psychology of Imagination*. New York, 1961

———. *Intimité* as *Intimacy*. In *Intimacy, and Other Stories*. New York, 1963

———. *M. François Mauriac et la liberté* as *François Mauriac and Freedom*. In *Literary and Philosophical Essays*. New York, 1955

———. *Les mains sales* as *Dirty Hands*. In *Three Plays*. New York, 1949

———. *La mort dans l'âme* as *Troubled Sleep*. New York, 1951

———. *Les mots* as *The Words*. New York, 1964

———. *Les mouches* as *The Flies*. In *No Exit & The Flies*. New York, 1947

———. *La nausée* as *Nausea*. Norfolk, Conn., 1949

———. *Nekrassov* as *Nekrassov*. In *The Devil & the Good Lord, and Two Other Plays*. New York, 1960

———. *Saint Genet, comédien et martyr* as *Saint Genet, Actor and Martyr*. New York, 1963

———. *Les séquestrés d'Altona* as *The Condemned of Altona*. New York, 1961

———. *Le sursis* as *The Reprieve*. New York, 1947

Schéhadé, Georges. *L'histoire de Vasco* as *Vasco*. In Robert Corrigan, ed., *New Theatre of Europe*, vol. 2. New York, 1964

Simenon, Georges. *Pedigree* as *Pedigree*. New York, 1963

Simon, Claude. *La bataille de Pharsale* as *The Battle of Pharsalus*. New York, 1971

———. *L'herbe* as *The Grass*. New York, 1960

———. *Histoire* as *Histoire*. London, 1969

———. *Le palace* as *The Palace*. New York, 1963

———. *La route des Flandres* as *The Flanders Road*. New York, 1961

———. *Le vent* as *The Wind*. New York, 1959

Sollers, Philippe. *Une curieuse solitude* as *A Strange Solitude*. New York, 1959

———. *Le parc* as *The Park*. London, 1968

Tardieu, Jean. *Il y avait foule au manoir* as *The Crowd up at the Manor*. In *The Underground Lover, and Other Experimental Plays*. London, 1968

Vailland, Roger. *Drôle de jeu* as *Playing with Fire*. London, 1948

Valéry, Paul. "*Mon Faust*" as "*My Faust*." In *Plays*, vol. 3 of *Collected Works*. New York, 1960

———. *Variété* as *Variety*. New York, 1927; *Variety: Second Series*. New York, 1938

Vercors. *La marche à l'étoile* as *Guiding Star*. In *Three Short Novels by Vercors*. Boston, 1947

———. *Le silence de la mer* as *The Silence of the Sea*. New York, 1944

Vian, Boris. *Les bâtisseurs d'empire* as *The Empire Builders*. New York, 1967

———. *L'écume des jours* as *Mood Indigo*. New York, 1968

———. *L'équarissage pour tous* as *The Knacker's ABC: A Paramilitary Vaudeville in One Long Act*. New York, 1968

Voltaire. *Candide* as *Candide*. New York, 1966

Weidlé, Wladimir. *Les abeilles d'Aristée* as *The Dilemma of the Arts*. London, 1948

Yourcenar, Marguerite. *Mémoires d'Hadrien* as *Memoirs of Hadrian*. New York, 1954

SECONDARY WORKS

Bibliographies and Guides

Boisdeffre, Pierre de, ed. *Dictionnaire de la littérature contemporaine*, 3rd ed. Paris, 1967
Bourin, André and Jean Rousselot. *Dictionnaire de la littérature française contemporaine*, 2nd ed. Paris, 1968
Braun, Sidney D. *Dictionary of French Literature*. New York, 1964
Cabeen, David C., ed. *A Critical Bibliography of French Literature*, 7 vols. Syracuse, N. Y., 1947ff.
Dictionnaire des auters français. Paris, 1961
Drevet, M. L. *Bibliographie de la littérature française, 1940–1949*. Geneva, 1955
Grente, G. and A. Pauphilet, eds. *Dictionnaire des lettres françaises*, 6 vols. Paris, 1951ff.
Harvey, Paul and J. E. Heseltine. *The Oxford Companion to French Literature*. Oxford, 1959
Klapp, Otto, ed. *Bibliographie der französischen Literaturwissenschaft*, 7 vols. Frankfurt, 1960ff.
Rousselot, Jean. *Dictionnaire de la poesie française contemporaine*, 2 vols. Paris, 1968

General Works

Albérès, René-Marill. *L'adventure intellectuelle du XXe siècle*. Paris, 1959
——. *Bilan littéraire du XXe siècle*. Paris, 1956
Bédier, Joseph and Paul Hazard. *Histoire de la littérature française illustrée*, 2 vols., 3rd. ed. Paris, 1952
Boisdeffre, Pierre de. *Métamorphose de la littérature*, 2nd. ed. Paris, 1963
Bouvier, Émile. *Les lettres françaises au XXe siècle*. Paris, 1962
Brée, Germaine and Margaret Guiton. *The French Novel from Gide to Camus*. New York, 1962
Brereton, Geoffrey. *A Short History of French Literature*. Baltimore, 1954
Brodin, Pierre. *Présences contemporaines: Littérature*, 3 vols. Paris, 1954–57

Cazaman, Louis. *A History of French Literature*. Oxford, 1955
Clouard, Henri. *Histoire de la littérature française du symbolisme à nos jours*. 2 vols., 2nd ed. Paris, 1960
————. *Petite histoire de la littérature française*. Paris, 1965
Curtius, Ernst Robert. *Französischer Geist im 20. Jahrhundert*, 2nd ed. Bern, 1960
Engler, Winfried. *Französische Literatur im 20. Jahrhundert*. Bern, 1968
————. *The French Novel from Eighteen Hundred to the Present*. New York, 1968
Grossvogel, David I. *20th Century French Drama*, 2nd ed. New York, 1961
Haedens, Kléber. *Une histoire de la littérature française*, 3rd ed. Paris, 1970
Hatzfeld, Helmut. *Trends and Styles in 20th Century French Literature*. Washington, D.C., 1966
Jan, Eduard von. *Französische Literaturgeschichte in Grundzügen*, 6th ed. Heidelberg, 1967
Krause, Gerd. *Tendenzen im französischen Romanschaffen des 20. Jahrhunderts*. Frankfurt, 1962
Lalou, René. *Le roman français depuis 1900*, 2nd ed. Paris, 1955
————. *Le théâtre en France depuis 1900*, 2nd ed. Paris, 1958
Lanson, Gustave and P. Truffau. *Manuel illustré d'histoire de la littérature française*, 3rd ed. Paris, 1957
Magny, Claude-Edmonde. *Histoire du roman française depuis 1918*, 2nd ed. Paris, 1956
Moore, Harry T. *Twentieth Century French Literature*, 2 vols. Carbondale, Ill., 1966
Pollmann, Leo. *Der französische Roman im 20. Jahrhundert*. Stuttgart, 1970
Rousseaux, A. *Littérature du XXe siècle*, 7 vols. Paris, 1952–61
Simon, Pierre-Henri. *Histoire de la littérature française au XXe siècle*, 2 vols., 8th ed. Paris, 1965
Theisen, Josef. *Geschichte der französischen Literatur*. Stuttgart, 1964
Turnell, Martin. *The Art of French Fiction*. New York, 1968

Works on Contemporary Literature

Albérès, René-Marill. *Histoire du roman moderne*. Paris, 1962
Beigbeder, Marc. *Le théâtre en France depuis la Libération*. Paris, 1959

Bernier, Michel Antoine. *Choice of Action: The French Existentialists in the Political Front Lines.* New York, 1968

Bersani, Jacques, et al. *La littérature en France depuis 1945.* Paris, 1970

Blanchot, Maurice. *Le livre à venir.* Paris, 1959

Boisdeffre, Pierre de. *Les écrivains français d'aujourd'hui.* Paris, 1963

———. *Une histoire vivante de la littérature d'aujourd'hui,* 7th ed. Paris, 1968

Butor, Michel. *Essais sur les modernes.* Paris, 1964

Chiari, Joseph. *Contemporary French Poetry.* Manchester, 1952

———. *The Contemporary French Theatre.* New York, 1959

Cruickshank, John, ed. *The Novelist as Philosopher: Studies in French Fiction 1935–1960.* London, 1962

Fletcher, John, ed. *Forces in Modern French Drama: Studies in Variations on the Permitted Lie.* New York, 1972

Fowlie, Wallace. *Climate of Violence.* New York, 1967

———. *Dionysus in Paris: A Guide to Contemporary French Theater.* New York, 1960

———. *A Guide to Contemporary French Literature.* New York, 1957

———. *Mid-century French Poets.* New York, 1955

Girard, Marcel. *Guide illustré de la littérature française moderne,* 3rd ed. Paris, 1962

Gmelin, Hermann. *Der französische Zyklenroman der Gegenwart.* Heidelberg, 1950

Grossvogel, David I. *The Self-conscious Stage in Modern French Drama.* New York, 1958

Guicharnaud, Jacques. *Modern French Theatre: From Giraudoux to Genet,* 2 vols., rev. ed. New Haven, Conn., 1967

Hobson, Harold. *The French Theatre of Today: An English View.* New York, 1965

Janvier, Ludovic. *Une parole exigeante: Le nouveau roman.* Paris, 1964

Lalou, René. *Histoire de la littérature française contemporaine,* 2 vols., 3rd ed. Paris, 1953

Lange, Wolf-Dieter, ed. *Französische Literatur der Gegenwart.* Stuttgart, 1971

Larnac, J. *La littérature française d'aujourd'hui.* Paris, 1948

Lesage, Laurent. *The French New Novel.* University Park, Pa., 1962

Mauriac, Claude. *The New Literature*. New York, 1959
Nadeau, Maurice. *The French Novel since the War*. New York, 1969
——. *Littérature presente*. Paris, 1952
Nathan, Jacques. *Histoire de la littérature française contemporaine, 1919–60*. Paris, 1964
Pabst, Walter, ed. *Das moderne französische Drama*. Berlin, 1971
——. *Der moderne französische Roman*. Berlin, 1968
Peyre, Henri. *French Novelists of Today*, 2nd ed. New York, 1967
Picon, Gaëtan. *Panorama de la nouvelle littérature française*, 3rd ed. Paris, 1968
Pingaud, Bernard, ed. *Écrivains d'aujourd'hui, 1940–1960: Dictionnaire anthologique et critique*. Paris, 1960
Pollmann, Leo. *Der Neue Roman in Frankreich und Lateinamerika*. Stuttgart, 1968
Pronko, Leonard Cabell. *Avant-Garde: The Experimental Theatre in France*. Berkeley, Cal., 1964
Raible, Wolfgang. *Die moderne Lyrik in Frankreich*. Stuttgart, 1972
Ricardou, Jean. *Problèmes du nouveau roman*. Paris, 1967
Richard, Jean-Pierre. *Onze études sur la poésie moderne*. Paris, 1964
Robbe-Grillet, Alain. *For a New Novel*. New York, 1966
Rousselot, Jean. *Panorama critique des nouveaux poètes français*. Paris, 1952
Sarraute, Nathalie. *The Age of Suspicion: Essays on the Novel*. New York, 1963
Serreau, Geneviève. *Histoire du nouveau théâtre*. Paris, 1966
Schöll, Konrad. *Das französische Drama seit dem zweiten Weltkrieg*, 2 vols. Göttingen, 1970
Zeltner-Neukomm, Gerda. *Das Wagnis des französischen Gegenwartsromans*. Hamburg, 1960

INDEX OF AUTHORS
AND PERIODICALS